D0836099

ST MARTIN'S
TRUE CRIME
CLASSICS

THEY LIVE BEHIND BARS . . .

KATHY: Friendly, disarming, and open about her violent past, she is known to her sister inmates as The Grandma. Her crime: murdering her bullying, drug-dealing husband.

PAULA: She seemed a loving mother whose life was beset with tragedy—until she claimed an intruder had snatched her newborn son.

JUDY: Petite and quiet, she looked like a deer caught in the headlights. But Judy hired a hitman to murder her husband, and in prison she was known as The Black Widow.

THEY KILLED TO GET THERE . . .

WOMEN BEHIND BARS

ST. MARTIN'S PAPERBACKS
TRUE CRIME LIBRARY TITLES
BY WENSLEY CLARKSON

Doctors of Death

Whatever Mother Says

Deadly Seduction

Slave Girls

Death at Every Stop

In the Name of Satan

Women Behind Bars

The Railroad Killer

The Mother's Day Murder

The Good Doctor

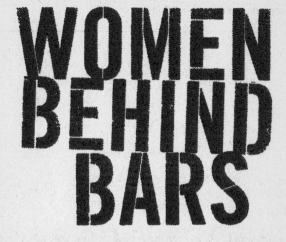

WOMEN BEHIND BARS

(PREVIOUSLY PUBLISHED AS *CAGED HEAT*)

WENSLEY CLARKSON

St. Martin's Paperbacks

Women Behind Bars was previously published under the title *Caged Heat*.

WOMEN BEHIND BARS

Copyright © 1998 by Wensley Clarkson.
Cover photograph by Ed Holub.

ISBN: 0-312-98111-2

Printed in the United States of America

St. Martin's Paperbacks edition / July 1998

10 9 8 7 6 5 4 3 2

For Shenée, Michelle, Kathy, and all the others who so graciously gave me their time

NOTES OF GRATITUDE

THE IDEA OF USING A LEADEN, DISPASSIONATE word like "acknowledgments" for this section cannot begin to express the depth of my feelings for the many individuals who have made this book possible. I owe them my deepest and most heartfelt gratitude.

First to my literary manager Peter Miller and my editor Charles Spicer. Without them this book would never have happened. Their support and guidance have been very much appreciated. Also many, many thanks to Uri and the rest of the team at PMA. Also, Rupert Maconick, who first suggested the idea of a book on this subject. His investigative skills have proved invaluable in helping me put this project together.

There are many inmates and staff at the three facilities primarily featured in this book who helped me. They include Shenée Green, Kathy Gaultney, Michelle Chapman, and all the others

I encountered during my travels across the country.

In New York, numerous associates have helped enormously, but a special debt of thanks goes out to Alex Burton who pointed me in the direction of Shenée Green and Bedford Hills. Also John Glatt for all the usual facilities, Pete Howlett, Jim Garrett, Patricia O'Connell, and Marion Collins at *The Star* and the staff of the New York Public Library.

In Illinois, Jeff Baker, Dylan Lambert, Rufus Stone, and Steve Moore helped furnish me with the sort of background material that is essential to a project like this.

In California there was Brendan Bourne, Anthony Bowman, Steve Shaw, Joe Paoella, and Mark Sandelson for all his amenities.

I spent four years researching and interviewing the women whose lives and crimes are described here. Often it was an emotionally painful experience to hear their stories, but I was struck by the indomitable spirit of so many female inmates compared to their male counterparts.

A few of the women featured here have been released since I encountered them, and one, tragically, has died. But even those facing the rest of their lives in prison showed great charm and humility throughout my dealings with them.

To them all I owe a huge note of thanks. They will not be forgotten . . .

The first prison I ever saw had inscribed on it "Cease to Do Evil: Learn to Do Well"; *but as the inscription was on the outside, the prisoners could not read it.*

—George Bernard Shaw

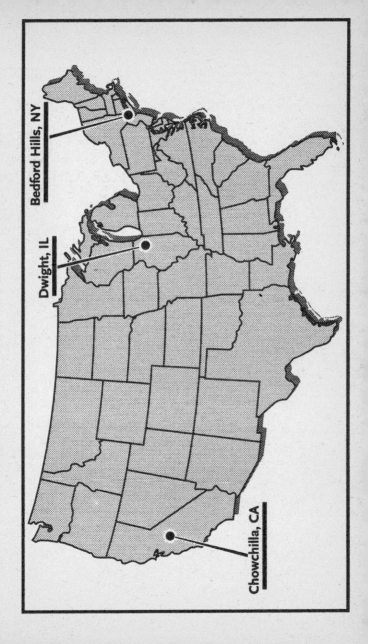

Introduction

IGNORE THE HOLLYWOOD VERSION OF *WOMEN Behind Bars*: sexy women parading through prison swinging their hips and turning up their noses at the world. On the big screen the good guys always win, which means they are set free. The fear, violence, and craziness only skim the surface, and the nightmare comes to a neat conclusion inside a couple of hours. Everyone lives happily ever after.

But the real-life females who reside in prisons across the nation offer a much bleaker picture. For many of them it is a lonely, tension-filled existence. A very grim reality.

Many of the women featured in this book have committed murder and face a very long time—if not their entire lives—in prison.

Home for them is an enclosed environment where money, sex, and drugs rule. The fortunate adjust by using whatever currency is available. The others suffer unimaginable humiliation.

The noise of prison is relentless. Twenty-four hours a day, remote-controlled locks clang open, women scream when their nightmares become too vivid, some moan softly with sexual ecstasy, others cry with hopelessness.

The moment these women have been sentenced, their lives take on a different significance. As they walk through the gates of prison they know they're marked for life.

The contrast with the freedom of the outside world is startling. Yet most prisons—including the ones featured in this book—aren't located in the inner ghettos or rundown projects from where so many crimes are committed. They're in quiet, isolated rural settings. That's where law-abiding citizens want them.

These prisons are spread out over acres of land and seem so quiet, serene, almost uninhabited. But this has no bearing on what goes on behind the razor-wired perimeters.

The officials who run these facilities—from the warden to the guards—have witnessed just about everything that involves the human species. Their job is to run these establishments coolly and professionally. Prisons are supposed to be orderly places, organized with careful precision because many hundreds of prisoners need to be housed, fed, and controlled. But even some staff members concede that often the rules have to be broken in order to keep the peace in such a volatile atmosphere.

At its best prison is functional and tolerable. At its worst it can be likened to a living nightmare where morals have long since disappeared and only the strong and shrewd can survive.

Many college-trained corrections managers insist that the days of barbaric conditions in U.S. prisons are over. Certainly, increasing numbers of states are building vast state-of-the-art facilities. But that doesn't change the faces of the inmates.

Whether there is an actual transformation, or an even partial rehabilitation of inmates while in prison remains a highly questionable point. Countless women leave prison even more likely to commit crimes than when they were originally incarcerated.

And many who seem strong, bright, and capable while behind bars find it virtually impossible to survive in the outside world after serving a lengthy sentence.

Ironically, despite their often heinous crimes, many of these women enjoy celebrity status within prison subculture. This can be due to the nature of their crime, efforts to foil the legal system, or simply the media attention their particular crime received. This so-called star status gives them a twisted kind of respect, unless the crime is detestable such as the murder and /or molestation of children. Then they are simply left to rot.

But beyond the criminal media stars, there are numerous other women criminals about whom we know far less. In every women's prison throughout the United States, there are tales of females who've strived to exist on the inside. There are few boundaries—morally or socially.

The secret of surviving a long sentence is finding a way to kill time. Some women become homosexual while in prison because the pursuit of sexual activity enables them to thrive in an often dangerous environment. Others pour themselves into educational studies—often trying to catch up with what they failed to achieve outside. But just as many others do absolutely nothing to help themselves.

Trying to cope with a hostile, meaningless existence drives many women over the edge. Some resort to violence as an expression of frustration. Others reach the edges of mental stability. Often their problems are not recognized until it is too late.

From the moment a woman convict goes through the gates and hears them close behind her, she knows that is it. For some, this may be the first time in their lives that they have been forced to stay somewhere they clearly do not want to be. They will be there until they have completed their sentence—''done their time.''

Certainly there are increasing numbers of inmates whose families have enough money for them to use it to hire a good lawyer, which means they might have a vague chance of beating the rap.

Meanwhile the rest of the families of the accused live with a faint hope that their loved ones might somehow escape justice. But, in reality, those chances are extremely slim.

Until quite recently there were very few convicted women criminals. Society protected females from the sort of conditions that encourage crime and there were things that most women just wouldn't do. There were also places that women did not venture.

Even when a female became involved in a serious crime, her male partners usually took the rap for them. And sometimes an attractive woman who actually ended up in court could influence a male judge and jury just by looking good.

In those days it was difficult for men to accept that women were even capable of serious crime.

So it is somewhat ironic that all the commendable strides that have been taken on behalf of women's rights in the latter half of this century have indirectly encouraged women to commit more serious crimes.

Female crime is now increasing at an alarming rate, fueled by a drastic increase in drug use and the cold hard fact that many women are now having to fend for themselves—and some of them, just like their male counterparts, cannot cope.

The role of male staff inside women's correctional facilities across the nation is highly controversial.

Some believe that allowing men to supervise female inmates is a vital development in today's so-called caring, sharing, sexually equal society.

Others—especially female inmates—believe that it is an invitation to men to be tempted into intimidating women and even sexually abusing prisoners on numerous occasions.

One male prison staff member says, "While I do not consider myself an expert on female offenders, I do believe I can offer valuable insight to male officers considering working in female facilities.'' The officer claims that many male prison staff openly assert that working in a women's facility is the last place they would advise anyone to work. But he says that such staff are clearly incapable of coping with the challenges faced in a women's facility.

''Let's set the record straight,'' says the officer. ''Working in a women's facility is a demanding job, one requiring as much professionalism as working in a men's facility. But that's the challenge.''

He claims the following myths surround men working in women's prisons:

- It is harmful to an officer's career to work in such a facility.

- There is a constant fear that a male officer will be accused of sexual misconduct.

- Female staff members will seek retribution for decades of oppression.

However, that same prison officer does concede: ''There are several important traits male staff must have to succeed in a women's prison. Male officers need a high level of professional competence, an awareness that they serve as role models, enough self-confidence to be able to take orders from female supervisors, and an understanding of the differences between male and female offenders.''

To understand these differences we must first

look at the environment many of the women came from. Most were dependent on men. Many were either abused or abandoned by men. Those who were abandoned were left with overwhelming problems to surmount—taking care of children, a lack of education, poor job skills, and low self-esteem.

Undoubtedly male offenders have different priorities from female offenders. The male prison environment is a macho world where the strong survive and the weak are victims.

Many male offenders even use the prison experience as an image enhancer. Prison is a tough place and they are tough guys. When they think about life after incarceration, male offenders are mostly concerned with money, cars, jobs, and partying.

The thoughts of the female offender, meanwhile, tend to be centered more on her children, her relationships, and her economic well-being. She does not have a macho image to fall back on to carry her through the tough times.

While these are generalizations—obviously, there are tough women inmates and there are male inmates who are concerned with their children—we should be aware that there are differences between male and female offenders, just as there are in free society. Before male staff can function properly in a women's facility, they have to recognize and be aware of these differences.

As one male officer admits, "It is a big adjustment to go from working in a men's facility. But professionally capable staff can make smooth transitions to different facilities regardless of the security level of the facility or whether it's male or female. Half of the battle is psychological—if you think it's going to be a negative experience, it will be.''

Male staff say there are two things that they must do in a female facility:

- Be professional. By doing this you will not have to be preoccupied with fears common to male staff about working in a women's prison.

- Work hard at being a positive role model. Many of these women have never really had a positive role model in their lives. This is the most important single impact male officers can have.

Adds one male prison officer, ''For men, working in a women's facility is a challenge. If you want to coast along until retirement, I would not recommend it. But if you're looking for a positive role in the system where a 'few good men' really can count, then you'll never regret the experience.''

The reaction of the female inmates is not surprising.

''Bullshit! The problem with having men working in women's prisons is that many of them are pussy-hunting all the time. I know that's why a lot of them volunteer to work in female facilities,'' says one prisoner. ''Sure there are exceptions. But I can tell you of at least five male officers carrying on sexual relations with inmates as we speak. It's all around us and it ain't ever goin' to go away.''

And the sexual innuendo between officers and inmates isn't all one way either.

Just walking through women's prisons it is clear that some female inmates are keen to catch the eye of any male—member of staff, reporter, whatever.

As one inmate concedes, ''Sure there are women here who want to have a ball with the male staff. They're frustrated, bored, lonely, what the hell d'you expect?

''We're not all bull dykes desperate for young meat. We have feelings, emotions, and urges just like women on the outside. Sometimes I wonder who the hell decided that men should work in women's prisons. It causes so much trouble. Many of the girls in this place are pretty, a lot of them are working girls who know just how to tempt a man.''

Some inmates are also convinced that certain male prison officers deliberately work in female facilities because they ''like the idea of women being under their command.'' One explains, ''I got no doubt about it. Some of the guys get a real kick out of orderin' us around and kickin' our butts. You can see it on their faces and in the bulge in their pants.''

The United States currently holds the dubious distinction of being first among industrialized nations in the rate at which we imprison our people.

By 1996 more than four million adults were

under the direction of some type of correctional agency. And while the rate of male imprisonment has increased by 116% during the past ten years, the female prison population increased by 210% during the same period.

The next century promises to see the figures rise even higher, especially given escalating public fear about crime and growing demand for incarceration and longer prison sentences.

But just who are these people who constitute one of the fastest-growing segments of our society? And what is it that makes women violent lawbreakers with a cold streak that often surprises even their male counterparts?

The obvious question begs to be asked: How many of these female criminals' sentences are influenced by the fact that they are women and often from a so-called minority race? On average, women criminals are set higher bail and get longer sentences.

Take the case of African-American Linda White, who was sentenced to 17 years to life for killing her abusive, drug-addicted boyfriend. In contrast, Robert Chambers, the "preppie murderer" who strangled his date, was given five to 15 years. In another mind-boggling sentence, Verdia Miller got 50 years to life for knowing about a murder her male friend committed, while he got 15 years.

Men who kill their partners serve less than one-third the prison time of women who kill their partners: two to six years compared with an average of 15 years for women. Eighty percent of women convicted for murdering a man state that they have been physically and/or sexually abused by that man.

A large number of the women featured in *Women Behind Bars* fit that profile.

Conditions are now changing toward even longer and harsher sentences. To some extent this seems to be a psychological shift, not a practical one.

In New York one attorney says, "The death penalty and longer sentences are really an empty gesture; it makes people feel better, but it's not going to affect the crime rate. Connecticut and New Jersey have had death penalty laws for 10 or 12 years and nobody has been executed yet. For punishment to have meaning it has to be swift and closely connected with the wrong."

In New York, where sentences must fall within certain minimum and maximum terms, murderers can plea bargain for 15-years-to-life. An overburdened court system saves money every time it allows a criminal to plea bargain, not only in the courts, but in the prisons where the state pays $25,694 a year for each inmate. There is an economic incentive to give prisoners reduced sentences.

Early records of prison reveal attitudes of extreme hatred and vengefulness toward offenders. An eye for an eye, a tooth for a tooth was the basic idea behind all punishment.

As for the extremely rare women offenders, usually they weren't even honored with a trial of any sort. Sometimes they were even thrown to the dogs, as was Jezebel of Old Testament times

(II Kings, Chapter 9). Other women were stoned for adultery, often by a group of men, including their own sexual partners.

In general the punishment was supposed to fit the crime. Guilt did not need to be proved if the lynch mob mentality ruled. This was Retribution with a capital R.

As times progressed an element of restitution crept into the so-called criminal justice system. A thief was expected to repay what he had stolen or give back something of equal or greater value. If he couldn't, then he would be ordered to work as a slave—possibly for many years.

But slowly and painfully people's thinking about crime and punishment began to change. Some began to question the wisdom of such punishments and this mood of self-examination continues to this day, particularly in regard to the death penalty.

But in general inmates still feel that retribution—or getting even—is still the first priority of any judge, jury, or police officer. This vein of suspicion runs throughout prisons—both male and female—and provides the background to most institutions. This air of suspicion creates tension between inmates and keepers.

No one can deny there have been numerous cases of rough treatment—sometimes even murder—at the hands of a custodial officer. It is often avoidable.

But the problem often lies with the lack of sympathy on both sides. The prison officer has a duty to control the actions of the lawbreaker.

And that can mean a strong, aggressive female

prisoner can make things very difficult for a custodial officer. Tensions rise and violence breaks out.

Many inmates simply don't know how to control their emotions and some have no wish to do so. There are prisoners who brag about their toughness.

"I got time 'cause I'm a mean bitch who kicked three cops when they tried to take me in. My crime meant nothin'. It was the hell I caused afterwards that got me in here," one inmate proudly says.

The truth is that there is a very thin line between "necessary control" and "unnecessarily rough treatment". That creates the atmosphere that can make or break prison life for inmates and their keepers.

Then there is the justice system's attempt at restitution. Repairing the damage, repaying what has been taken. The problem is, as most of the women featured in this book prove, what purpose can possibly be served by executing a murderer? The victim cannot be restored to life. Certainly, society must be protected from other killings committed by the murderer. But how can this be guaranteed, even inside prison? Can the punishment really be made to fit the crime?

These days, the prison system across the nation has been actively geared against retribution and for rehabilitation. This doesn't necessarily mean it's working, for no one has yet come up with the magic answers. But the goal now is to release some women prepared to start a new, constructive life that will never again lead them into trouble. It doesn't work in a lot of cases.

Much of the reason for the crime boom among women centers around the so-called "war babies" of the 1940s who reached their twenties and thirties in the sixties and seventies. The high birthrate of those years is well reflected in the higher crime rates. Family controls weakened as those children were growing up, resulting in a greater number of violent crimes committed by very young people.

For many years before this, prisons housed women inmates with an average age of 30 to 35. That average has today dropped to around 22. The movement of poorer people to the big cities in the seventies and early eighties also had a very detrimental effect.

Compounding this problem today is that the children of those war babies are now grown up and getting involved in even more crime than their parents.

Some still recommend the "lock 'em up and throw away the key" solution. But that would mean literally hundreds of new prisons being built across the nation.

The woman felon must want to change her lifestyle if the correctional system is going to work. If she simply drifts back to her old criminal associates then chances are she'll be back in jail very swiftly. She must want rehabilitation.

But does such a prisoner really want to rebuild her life? Does she want to change her ways, her attitudes, even her home in order to start a law-abiding life?

Nearly all the women I spoke to for this book

insisted that they did want to rebuild their lives. But then they know that they have to say that to the parole board if they are to stand any chance of an early release.

One ex-con makes a very clear definition of what rehabilitation really means: "You gotta be totally crime-free. That means no drugs, no stealin', no law-breakin' lovers. If someone you know from the past comes up to you in the street, walk away. Don't get involved. It's up to you."

So what's the story of women in prison? Who are they? Where do they come from? Why are they in prison? What's a woman's life really like inside?

In this book I have focused on women who have committed very serious crimes; they are the ones who live, eat, and breathe in the prisons for a very long time—sometimes for the rest of their lives. They are the ones who have time to reflect on their crimes, reflect on life inside. They are the ones who notice every detail.

Perhaps this book will make it possible to better understand the female criminal psyche. It certainly will provide a glimpse inside three of the biggest women's prisons in the world. These are microsocieties within society. The women inmates share the same emotional ups and downs as the rest of us, but for them there is no escape from the reality of their predicament.

Many of these inmates have a very personal knowledge of other similar institutions, sometimes across the nation. Many have already been through juvenile training or correctional centers during their teen years. They may even have been in special schools for young girl offenders, narcotics- or alcohol-treatment facilities, mental institutions, county jails, and even other federal prisons.

As with any other group, a women's prison population consists of a wide variety of people. Some are highly articulate, artistic, friendly, even easy to talk to. These are the ones who tend to be very well aware of the problems of life inside. They often accept personal responsibility for being in prison.

Others are bitter and hostile toward everyone while some are simply dull, emotionally disturbed, lacking motivation to improve their lot, uncommunicative, and unwilling to accept any blame for their predicament.

One of the women featured in this book at first only agreed to speak to me if I guaranteed her anonymity. She said she wanted to protect her family. I agreed.

Then one month after meeting her inside, I received a letter from her saying she'd changed her mind and was so proud of her attempts at rehabilitation and the beautiful young daughter she had produced that she wanted her real name to appear. She was one of the brave ones.

The basis of this book is that it features real women, all of whom share the experience of being prisoners. From the first bell in the morning to the clang of the automatic door bars at night lockup, their day is planned for them. Every move they make is anticipated or rapidly probed.

What happens to a woman when she first arrives at prison? It all depends on the individual policy routine at a particular prison. But certain things occur to all of them, no matter who they are or why they are there.

There aren't many happy endings for the sort of women featured in *Women Behind Bars*. Many are doomed to live out the rest of their lives in prison waiting in terror for that dark, airless day when they finally meet their maker. The few who do get released will often never recover from the aftereffects of their crimes, the guilt, and the anguish of serving a long prison sentence.

Suicide is still a regular occurrence inside women's prisons. Many inmates are haunted by the sight of an inmate with blood dripping from her wrists or hanging from an overhead beam. Some prison staff take the attitude that such deaths save the taxpayer the tens of thousands of dollars it costs to feed and accommodate a murderer. Others call it a criminal waste of a human life.

Many inmates claim that the staff treat them like animals. Some even say that guards often turn the other way when violence flares.

The truth is that nobody walks out of prison unscathed. The lucky ones return to their families and pick up the shreds of their former lives. Others trust no one and take to the road, constantly drifting from place to place. And of course there are the ones who will never be released.

One long-term inmate I befriended—Shenée Green—summed it up in a poem she recently wrote for me:

I lay here alone, feeling confused, out of touch, unwanted, unloved, singly alone.

When I lay awake on a sleepless night (which is quite often) I think of all I feel and reality grips me, and once again I know and feel all alone.

A daytime activity for me is—fastforward— so that I might only think at night, think of being alone ...

On a regular day, (which is everyday) I put on the mask of happiness helping others, hoping someone can see my mask and know how to help me.

I refuse to reveal my real self to others, because to do that, I might later regret it, so again this vicious circle continues, feeling alone ...

Sitting in this prison cell, I always tend to reflect on past errors, the people I've encountered, and not knowing how to enjoy the minute, joy in my short life.

Until this "very" day, I still don't fully understand why I torture myself with past thoughts. Maybe in time I shall, but as it stands I'm confined with life (in prison), wanting so much, and yet feeling so alone ...

Prologue

SHE ARRIVES IN A SPECIAL BUS UNDER HEAVY guard. She's cuffed. She is seated between two beefy custody officers, one of whom is a woman. They are responsible for getting the prisoner to the next set of officers. They watch her every move. They cannot relax for one moment and the stony look on their faces say it all.

The first gate they enter in the prison is called the sally port. The officer in charge identifies him- or herself, and the bus creeps forward to the second gate. The same thing happens there. When that second gate shuts, the free world is completely gone.

The bus then stops at the Reception Guidance Center—RGC—where the admission routine begins. If it's late at night and the new prisoner is considered dangerous then some of the admissions process may be left until the following day.

Then the "body receipt" is signed by the lady officer at the RGC desk. This states that the officers have delivered the prisoner in safe condition to the officer in charge.

The custody officer at RGC tells her to remove all her jewelry and to hand over the few personal possessions she has brought. They will be returned to her later. Everything is carefully listed, and she signs the list before her belongings are taken away in a basket. Those things were important to her because they made her feel a bit different, a little special. But now they're all gone. She is only allowed to keep her watch if it is plain and not too valuable; otherwise it could help her bribe anyone on the inside.

Because of the seriousness of her offense she is then body-searched. This will include a thorough vaginal and anal examination.

Next comes a shower, including a shampoo. Then she will be given prison-issue clothes and bedding. If her commitment papers show she has tried to harm herself or others or has been rebellious in a physical manner, she may be given a "strong dress" and a "strong blanket." These are made of material so tough that it cannot be torn by hand.

A room in RGC is then assigned to her. If she needs special medical or psychiatric treatment she may be kept in RGC much longer. That room—usually about six feet by nine feet—will have a small lavatory concealed by a cushion top, a little table for bathroom articles, writing paper, pictures, etc. There will be a small closet to hang a few clothes full-length. A long narrow slit in the door to her room will enable a supervisor to look in at any time, day or night.

During the following days and weeks in RGC she has to go through many routines. First of all there is a complete medical examination performed by a doctor and nurse. She is checked for physical problems as well as AIDS, venereal disease, tuberculosis, diabetes, and other chronic illnesses. Careful records are made of any track marks that indicate intravenous drug use. Tattoos, scars, facial problems of various kinds, skin abrasions, and any crippling deformities are examined. Relevant entries are made on her record by the medics.

Following the medical examination, she will undergo various other tests, some of them by the psychiatric treatment unit. The results of these will be used to determine the need for special treatment or individual counselling.

Then come the educational tests. Many inmates claim better education than they have in fact received. They later claim these tests had bad results because they were still too upset about being sentenced to prison.

The new inmate is then assigned a counselor. How much time is spent with the inmate depends on the case load facing that particular counselor. But the purpose of the counselor is to provide a bridge to the prison staff.

The inmate is also to be helped to choose an educational goal or some other field of vocational training. However, some prisoners refuse all offers of help and remain hostile throughout.

Some counselors are excellent, some are useless and swamped by as many personal problems

as the very inmates they are supposed to be helping.

Back in her room, the prisoner is given a
folder of documents of typewritten notes of the
rules of the facility, the commissary hours, visiting privileges, and regulations about what can
be sent to her by her family or friends and what
items are forbidden. From this day on for as long
as she is in prison she must live by those rules.

She is now a "fish," a prison newcomer,
ready to be tried out by her fellow inmates. She
will be assigned a job and caught up in the routine of the institution. She may well be rebellious
and hostile, submissive and docile, whatever
mood suits the moment.

She will rapidly discover that the inmate code
exists in every prison. Others will try to find out
where she stands on a vast range of subjects. The
only exceptions to this are the women sentenced
to death. They are the untouchables, confined to
their maximum-security unit under constant
guard. They are only rarely in contact with the
rest of the prison population.

Inside prison there is a strict social structure
that can be as hard to crack as any exclusive club
in the outside world. Other inmates want the fish
to fit into their structure, to find out if she is of
any use to them. She will go through many tests
before she is accepted.

The first big question is how does she stand
on snitching, the greatest inmate crime of all? If
she isn't on their side then they'll completely cut
her out. She can never be trusted with inside in-

formation. The most popular testing place is in the first meal lineup.

The line begins to form an hour before the meal is served. Most inmates look forward to the dinner hour because the food is just about worth eating and it's a prime opportunity for socializing. Most women's prisons allow a certain flexibility at meal time. The women sit at tables with their special friends in groups of four to six. Any woman who barges in on these gatherings is likely to be rebuffed. But if she's invited to come in then that's okay.

The testing of the fish includes detailed questioning about her sexuality. A gay inmate might be urged to try and seduce her just to see if she is that way inclined.

It is impossible to provide any serious figures on the extent of homosexuality within the women's prison system, but undoubtedly a large number of inmates and staff are lesbians. Some prisoners reckon that up to 90% of female inmates have some sort of homosexual experience while in prison.

"Some are gay before they come in," says one long-term inmate. "In some ways it's easier for them. But then there are the others who just get desperate for some kinda sex, to feel another human body real close, see if it's warm. If that makes us gay then I guess most of us in here are."

The testing of the fish continues. She's too fresh to be taken into everyone's confidence, but if she plays her cards right she'll get on board with the majority of inmates. The best attitude seems to be, "You do your time, I'll do mine."

Some inmates quite happily enter into sexual relationships with staff members—both male and female—because it gets them special privileges.

But whatever slot the fish settles into in prison she will be expected to serve her time without causing trouble. She will never be allowed to step out of it for one moment, not even if she becomes a leader of inmates herself, a recognized tester of other fish.

During the period inside the RGC a new inmate is confined to medium security unless she has a history of violent behavior, in which case she will be held in a maximum-security room until she is able to discipline herself to life in medium security.

The next degree of confinement is called close custody, which is not quite as serious as maximum security. The inmate has to be accompanied by a custody officer at all times. That includes meals in the dining room and counseling-group sessions. Most prisoners are under medium security and can participate in most activities within the prison.

But one of the first things a new inmate needs to know is just where the lines are drawn. Is it very strict? Are they flexible? Which staff members are hard? Who is soft? Conversations with other inmates will provide the answers most of the time.

During the first few weeks in prison, the new inmate will feel terribly cut off from all she has known. Loss of personal privacy and unannounced room searches (shakedowns) or eyes

peering at her through a slot in the door at countless times are very intrusive.

Only after that initial assessment will she be assigned a cell in the main prison.

PART ONE

Bedford Hills Correctional Facility,
New York

THE ROAD TO BEDFORD HILLS TWISTS AND
turns down into a small valley among the leafy
communities of one of New York's most affluent
suburbs. From a distance it looks like a nonde-
script, untidy collection of cinderblock and red
brick outhouses. But the 15-foot-tall, touch-
sensitive steel-gray fences that encircle the compound soon catch the eye.

Squat brick buildings litter the prison area.
From a gray watchtower just behind the main
gates, three uniformed officers observe approaching visitors through a smoked glass screen.

At 10:00 A.M. the pathways between the main
cell-block buildings are crowded with women
wielding brooms, rakes, and paint brushes, many
wearing informal, brightly colored shirts and
dresses that contrast starkly with the blue-and-

black uniforms of the officers who move among them.

More than 30% of the 700 inmates at Bedford have been convicted of capital offenses—murder, conspiracy to murder, and kidnapping being the most common.

In New York State, Bedford is supposed to house all females whose sentences require maximum security. But it is dwarfed by its male counterparts such as Sing Sing and Attica.

There are also many differences from those grim, soulless men's institutions; no dogs, no sharpshooters taking aim with high-velocity rifles from watchtowers positioned on every corner.

The lone officer sitting in an attendant's booth at the main gate even smiles pleasantly as visitors' IDs are casually checked.

Inside the front gate, the walls acquire an institutional yellow and gray as that air of pleasant informality rapidly disappears.

Visitors are immediately frisked and then stroked menacingly with a large metal detector that sends alarms coursing through the bleak hallway area identifying pens, eyeglass frames, shoelace eyelets on boots, bras, corsets, garters.

Pockets are emptied; hats, belts, and shoes removed.

In the prison visitor's manual a strict dress code states: "All adults entering the facility must be properly dressed and appropriately attired covering all the body. Example: No halter tops, bared midriffs, very short skirts or very short shorts, see-through clothing, etc. You are allowed to bring your coat into the visiting area.''

Then as an afterthought: ''This dress code applies to adults, not to children.''

All personal items have to be placed in the visitor's locker area provided at the front gate at a cost of 25 cents. The staff make a point of saying, ''Your quarter will be returned when you take your items out upon leaving the facility.''

Pampers, baby formula, bottles, and baby food are allowed. But no strollers or carriages are permitted.

A wait of some minutes follows as phone calls are made, driver's licenses checked, questions asked, and then the filing system is opened on a yellowing desktop computer that splutters into life.

All visitors have to complete a visiting pass using the inmate's full name and her departmental identification number. The pass must also include the visitor's name, address, and relationship to the inmate they are visiting.

On the wall is a warning to any visitors under 18 years of age: *Unmarried minors under 18 years of age must have prior written permission from their parents or guardian to visit an inmate who is NOT a relative. The written permission may be mailed to the counselor in advance or presented by the accompanying adult at the time of the visit.*

Visitors wishing to leave money for an inmate on the date of the visit have to do so prior to entering the visiting room. At a vast high-standing desk the administration lobby officer provides a receipt for the specific amount left for the inmate. There is a $50 limit.

Visitors to Bedford Hills inmates are processed on a strictly first come, first served basis. The visiting room opens at 8:30 A.M. daily. Visiting ends at 3:30 P.M. daily.

There are strict rules about so-called "cross-visiting". This is when two inmates have a visit with one or more visitor. This is only permitted with the written approval of the prison superintendent, but it is encouraged among immediate family members of inmates.

But the visiting room guidelines at Bedford make their point loud and clear:

1. Visits will be immediately terminated if departmental rules are not followed to the word.

2. Inmates and visitors are not to leave the visiting room area together. They must even use separate bathrooms.

3. Inmates are not allowed to use the vending machines in the visiting room. They are also forbidden from using the microwave oven or handling money.

4. In general, kissing, embracing, and touching are allowed as long as it is acceptable behavior in a public place and does not offend others present. Physical contact cannot embarrass young children. Prolonged kissing or "necking" is not allowed. But physical bonding between mother and child is encouraged.

5. A visitor and an inmate may hold hands, as long as their hands are in plain view of others. Inmates and visitors sitting next to one another may also rest their hands upon each others' shoulder or around each others' waists.

6. Aggressive physical contact such as hitting, pushing, or striking is not tolerated. This includes disciplining children. Any such physical contact will result in immediate termination of the visit.

7. Loud, abusive, or boisterous actions, disruptive or argumentative behavior, or sexual activities which constitute unacceptable physical contact will mean visiting privileges will be revoked.

8. A visitor or inmate who appears to be under the influence of alcohol or drugs during a visit will also mean visiting privileges revoked.

9. When a visitor or inmate attempts to introduce or pass contraband, or any item, privileges will be revoked.

The doors to the cells inside Bedford open at 6 A.M. and slam shut at 10:30 P.M. There are four major body counts a day and during each of them the prisoners are expected to stay exactly where they are so as to be accounted for.

Every inmate works and they are paid about $15 every two weeks.

As one prisoner explains: "The food is pretty bad, but we do often get to cook ourselves and many of us eat in groups. Also relatives and friends send in food as well. We had turkey at Christmas—big deal.''

On the other side of the fence—literally—is Bedford Hills superintendent Elaine A. Lord. She is the matriarchal figure who seems to combine toughness with a pleasant touch.

Many of the women pour their hearts out to Ms. Lord when she makes her daily rounds of the facility. She is understandably proud of the fact that Bedford Hills has a prison nursery where infants spend the first year of their lives with inmate mothers.

Inside a facility the size of Bedford Hills there are also other important concerns like the problem of the mentally ill, the numerous victims of such traumas as incest, batterings, and rape.

The whole mix is here. The atmosphere swings from intimidating to relaxed. The expressions on the inmates' faces say it all: misery, contempt, emptiness, merry self-denial. It's a tough place where only the strong survive.

ONE

Shenée

SHENÉE GREEN—INMATE NUMBER 91G2200—has been in prison seven years for her part in the brutal murder of an old woman during an alleged robbery attempt. She has always denied being a killer.

Shenée has haunted me from the first moment I saw her in the visiting room at Bedford on Friday, June 13, 1997. She is 27 years old. Her dark brown curly hair cascades down onto her shoulders. She is wearing brand-new white sneakers, blue shirt and pants. A few freckles on her brown cheeks are the only clue to her half Italian ancestry, which she says greatly hindered her early childhood. "No one accepted me. I wasn't black or white."

Shenée is quite beautiful, but more than beautiful—she has a hypnotic brand of sweetness that makes it hard to concentrate on what she is saying.

She talked in eloquent, emotive terms about her life inside prison and the harsh world she left behind on the streets near her home in the projects of midstate New York.

As Shenée spoke it was as if she was sitting on an empty stage lit by a single, bare bulb. "I gotta survive, but I don't see no light at the end of the tunnel. I may look young still, but inside I'm one old bitch!"

Shenée has almost 20 years to go on a sentence of 28-and-a-half-to-life. What does that sentence look like from the inside where prison authorities are cutting inmate programs intended to rehabilitate mind and body—from exercise equipment to college education?

"I fuckin' hate it in this place. When I got here I just about hated everyone else, too. I thought everythin' was my own fault. I'd brought all this on myself. There were times when I wanted to end it all. Some days I felt like the cell doors might never open again the next morning. But that's what it feels like."

Shenée was born into poverty and hardship. She portrays herself as a victim of neglect and abuse.

"Both my parents left me alone a lot. They caused a lot of the bad things in my life. If it wasn't for them I probably wouldn't be here."

Shenée has a child—born just a few months before her incarceration. Shenée says the child was the result of being raped by her boyfriend.

"That's why I'm so scared for my baby. I only want the best for her. I don't want her to end up like me. I think about my daughter all the time. I'm so desperate to be with her. She's the only reason I stay alive really. I fought for visitation rights to her. My mom tried to keep her away from me.

"I'm always havin' words with my mom about her. It tears me apart to think about it all and I'm so scared my mom will do to her what she did to me. My mother robbed me of my childhood, and now prison is robbing me of my child."

Shenée is often "put in the box" for bad behavior. She's also been written a lot of disciplinary tickets, which mean a $5 fine. But the core of her problems lie with her own terror about being institutionalized. "I want to have a life when I get out, but I'm scared that I won't be able to cope when it finally happens."

Shenée fights a constant battle within herself. In many ways it's harder than dealing with all the day-to-day physical problems of being in prison.

"You want to know what a day is like in here? It's humiliatin', scary, and exhausting. I cannot wait for each day to end, so I can go to sleep. I don't care 'bout the nightmares 'cause nothin' can compare with reality—that's the real nightmare."

Shenée's real-life "nightmare" began on April 27, 1991, when she was arrested for a robbery. Then she was accused of another robbery and of murdering a 78-year-old woman who lived next door to an apartment Shenée shared with a lover called Larkia Barnett.

The following day the old lady's body was discovered. On May 10, 1991, Shenée was charged with the murder and two counts of burglary.

Shenée was found guilty on October 22, 1991, and the following month was sentenced to 28-and-half-years-to-life.

She arrived at Bedford Hills on December 17, 1991. Like so many other inmates she still insists she is innocent.

"It was circumstantial evidence, no murder weapon, no eyewitness, no fingerprints, no nothin' . . . I did this shit to myself. In the long run I have suffered, day in, day out."

Shenée believes in the essential prison code of respect. It's imperative to her and in the past she hasn't hesitated to fight other inmates who've "dissed" her.

"For seven years I've fought other inmates because I've hurt so bad, and they disrespected me, or at least that's what I felt. I have always felt that if you have nothing else in prison, you must have your respect."

When I first visited Shenée she didn't want me to use her real name for fear of retribution inside Bedford Hills. Then she changed her mind. "I want you to use my real name. They can't do anything more to me. It cannot get any worse! I've got nothin' to hide no more."

Currently Shenée is trying to get the legal right to remove her daughter from the custody of her mother, whom she still blames for her troubled life.

Yet Shenée still managed to have time to think of others. Even the death of Princess Diana had a profound effect.

"Sad shit, huh? What a fucked up way to go, and I know her two sons are taking it very hard. I watched the funeral on television. I never met her, and I even cried, because it was such a waste."

It is claimed that at least one senior member of staff at Bedford Hills is living with another woman on the grounds of the prison. That lover actually had a job inside the prison until a credit card scam was uncovered at the facility and security checks revealed the woman was an ex-con.

"They try to keep a lid on the happenings inside these prison walls, but we always find out in the end. The staff gossip just as much as us," says Shenée.

So-called celebrity inmates also get a lot of coverage from the Bedford Hills gossips. But then they are the equivalent of Hollywood inside any facility.

Says Shenée, "I've had many encounters with so-called famous prisoners. There's one who spends the whole time talkin' about her escape plan. I think she'll do it in the end. She manipulates the administration very well. That's the key to success here—manipulation." Significantly, Shenée refuses to name the prisoner. She proudly says she is "no snitch."

During her incarceration, Shenée has even had sexual relations with a member of the prison staff. "I need sex. That's the way it is in here. It helps you survive in a place like this. I guess that was my version of manipulation."

Shenée was very close to two other inmates,

but they were more for comfort than sexual gratification. "That's the way it is in here. You need someone to hold, someone to cry with, someone to make love to. I got urges like everyone else."

When she entered prison Shenée weighed 300 pounds. But a diet of illicit drugs helped her to cure her obesity and she's slimmed down. Drugs are an everyday part of life inside Bedford.

"They come in through visitor's mouths, shoes, vagina, assholes, you name it—and they are always around."

One of Shenée's closest friends inside Bedford is one of the facility's most beautiful inmates, Donna Hylton. It's said that she's lusted after by more than half the other prisoners.

Donna is serving 25-years-to-life for her part as an accessory to the gruesome murder of a man.

GIRL GANG SEIZED IN TRUNK SLAYING screamed the headlines on April 8, 1985, when Donna was arrested. She was eventually found guilty of taking part in the brutal torture and murder of 63-year-old Long Island real-estate broker Thomas Vigliarole.

Vigliarole died because his partner in crime, Louis Miranda, thought Vigliarole had swindled him out of $139,000 from a deception they had pulled off together.

Donna and two girlfriends, Rita and Theresa, were invited to participate in the crime by the girlfriend of the man hired to do the killing. Their cut was going to be $9,000 each. Donna wanted the money to pay for a photo portfolio to help her break into modelling.

Vigliarole was lured into believing the three girls were prostitutes. On March 8, 1985, they picked him up, drugged him and then drove him to one of the girls' apartments in Harlem already kitted out with torture equipment. The closet door had been cut, a pot put in it for use as a toilet and the windows boarded up.

Over the next 15 to 20 days, Vigliarole was starved, tortured, burned, beaten, and sexually assaulted, including having a three-foot metal bar pushed up his rectum. One of the accused was later asked why they had presumed Vigliarole was homosexual. "When I stuck the bar up he wiggled," came the response.

Donna Hylton was assigned the task of delivering the ransom note and a tape to a friend of Vigliarole, who managed to get a partial license plate number from her car. Donna and the rest of the gang were eventually traced by police.

One investigator says, "I couldn't believe this girl who was so intelligent and nice looking could be so unemotional about what she was telling me she and her friends had done. They'd squeezed the victim's testicles with a pair of pliers, beat him, burned him. Actually, I thought the judge's sentence was lenient."

Donna's signed statement and the recollections of investigators clearly implied she was a willing participant in the kidnaping and killing of Vigliarole.

"All the girls' hairs were on the bedsheet they wrapped him in," recalled one detective. "So they were all on the bed with him, or maybe having sex with him."

Today, Donna Hylton insists that when she was a child she was the victim of regular abuse. She also claimed she was sexually molested by a female neighbor who babysat her. She later discovered the same woman was having a relationship with her stepfather.

Donna also claims one of her teachers at school molested her and that was when she concluded that nobody would love her. They just all wanted to use her for sex. That feeling has never gone away. It sounds like a cry for help. But is it too late?

Life in jail holds many fears for Donna Hylton. But the overriding one is that she'll die in custody.

"There was a woman here everybody talks about," says Donna. "She was named Ma Brown and came here when this prison was a farm, and people used a horse and buggy.

"They gave her a life sentence for murder. After 25 years they commuted her sentence and she got out. She stayed out a month or two and asked to come back. She'd come in one century and left in another, and she was too scared.

"She would rather end up dying here. God, I don't want to end up like Ma Brown."

The fears and tribulations of the Bedford Hills inmates are often overshadowed by the public sagas of celebrity inmates like Amy Fisher . . .

TWO
Amy

THEN THERE IS THE SO-CALLED "LONG ISLAND Lolita"—Amy Fisher. She's been shuttling between Bedford Hills and Albion Prison ever since being sentenced to 5-to-15 years for shooting the wife of her older lover in 1992. Only a few weeks after being incarcerated she fell in love with a female inmate who was a beautician in the prison's L-Block.

Amy sneaked into the woman inmate's cubicle for regular sex sessions.

"It's easy if you don't make any noise—I crawl real low on my hands and knees so that the corrections officer on duty can't see me from behind his desk," Amy later explained.

The object of Amy Fisher's desires was a convicted killer in her early thirties who had already served more than eight years for slaying two people. "This other woman became very protective of Amy and stopped other inmates from hassling her," explains one inmate.

Then Amy even tried to recruit another inmate to arrange a bizarre "wedding" ceremony with her illicit lover. "I want to marry her and be with her forever," Amy told the other inmate. "Can I buy a couple of rings and have them sent here in your name?"

Inmates were only allowed to have a small amount of jewelry at Albion, and Amy had already reached her limit, so she wanted the other inmate to claim ownership of the rings.

But Amy's relationship came to an abrupt end when the other woman became eligible for a work-release program in New York City.

"I can't believe she's going—I don't want her to go," Amy despaired to another inmate at the time. "I don't know what I'm gonna do when she's not here."

But predatory inmates like Amy don't go for long without sex.

One hot summer's night in June, 1993, she enjoyed a steamy sex session in the shower with a 50-year-old lesbian.

Amy even later admitted to a friend, "I was feeling real horny. She was always coming onto me, so I just wanted to get it over with."

Amy's behavior then got even more out of control. Rumors began spreading around Albion Prison that the Long Island Lolita had got pregnant by one of the male prison guards.

The officer—who was twice Amy's age—later denied being involved with the teenager, although Amy insisted she had the fling because she "needed sex."

At 6 A.M. on September 8, 1993, Amy was transferred back to Bedford Hills.

Despite all this some of the other inmates insist she is basically a good person.

"Amy was known as a real sex freak, but people shouldn't look down on her because of the wild action she was taking part in. There were 900 inmates—all female—when Amy and I were there, and you just know that most of the male prison guards were taking advantage of the situation," recalls one ex-inmate. "About 90% of the inmates were gay, and others who had never been gay in their life—like Amy—had to join in just to survive. It's hard for someone who's never been in prison to understand."

As a so-called celebrity inmate, Amy became the center of attention among other inmates from the moment she first arrived at the facility.

"She really looked cute," says one of her closest pals. "She was wearing expensive sneakers, a sweatshirt with a hooded top, and she had her ugly green pants tapered tight down her legs by twisting them and then rolling up the bottoms—you're not allowed to alter your pants with a needle and thread.

"She was also wearing lipstick and mascara, and had her hair up in a high ponytail. When Amy walked around the prison, she always kept herself looking good. She always looked like a million dollars and everybody noticed, male and female."

Amy Fisher's daily routine began at 7 A.M. when all inmates are expected to be awake, dressed, and ready for breakfast, which usually includes hot cereal or an eight-ounce scoop of scrambled eggs, and juice and toast.

Work detail lasts from 8 A.M. until 4 P.M. with a break for lunch—meat (beef or cheap cuts of poultry), soup and vegetables—at 11:30 A.M.

Dinner at 5 P.M. is beef teriyaki or spaghetti, with specialties like chicken once a week and pork chops once a month. Inmates also have the option of cooking on their unit's hot plate, with food received in packages, rather than eat the prison fare.

But Amy Fisher was a picky eater who didn't spend much time dining in the mess hall. She even managed to get a lot of health food sent to her from home. "I'd rather eat nuts and cereals than what this place is serving," she told one inmate.

Amy's schedule allowed her to visit the recreation area—to play pool or workout in the gym—from 6:30 to 7:30 P.M. All inmates have to be in bed for lockup and lights out at 10:30 P.M.

Amy didn't watch much TV or workout much during her free time. She preferred to spend more time around her room. But then she had a lot more nice things than most inmates—burgundy silk sheets, cooking pans, plush towels, loads of nice clothes. As one inmate explains, "She just calls her lawyer, and he puts money into her account."

But as a celebrity inmate Amy is a magnet for trouble—especially at the hands of the prison guards, who regularly gave her disciplinary tickets which result in a week or more in solitary lockup.

Amy believed she was getting a raw deal. "One time they called my unit to go to work, and I wanted to take a minute to blow-dry my hair," she told one prison pal. "It was 20 degrees below zero outside and I had to walk outdoors from my dorm to the mess hall. I didn't refuse to work—they're just looking to bust my chops all the time."

On another occasion Amy was involved in an argument with two male correctional officers in the prison mess hall because each had told her to do her job a different way. "If one of you tells me to do it this way, and the other tells me to do it that way, whichever way I do it, I'm gonna be wrong!" she told them before walking away from the argument. Amy was immediately disciplined for insubordination.

Amy was angry because prison authorities had been giving her lowly jobs in the mess hall—sweeping, mopping, cleaning the toilets. She often hid in a bathroom when she was trying to get out of a job. As one inmate kept telling her, "You're not gonna make it with an attitude like this."

As another inmate explains, "It was hard to put Amy on any job where she had to interact with the other inmates because most of them really loved to pick on her."

Amy's refusal to work landed her in solitary lock down for a week. "Just a bunk, a toilet, and nothing else with your meals eaten in," explains one inmate.

When Amy got out she was moved to a new dorm, but she continued to cause problems. From that moment on prison staff moved her every couple of months.

It took Amy many months before she realized she had to toe the line. Eventually she got a friend who ran the prison bakery to help get her a job there, too.

Amy was told she would really have to work—no shirking off. Amy promised she'd behave and was given a two-week trial. She turned out to be one of the best bakers the facility ever had.

Throughout this period, Amy Fisher looked forward most of all to the regular visits by her beloved mother, Rose.

"I can tell my mother anything because she's my best friend," Amy told one prison pal.

Amy's mother visited at least once a month, and Amy phoned her every single night from the facility.

Inside Bedford Hills, Amy Fisher's growing resentment towards men manifested itself in her overt criticism of Joey Buttafuoco, the lover who provoked Amy's attack on his own wife Mary Jo.

Amy told her prison pal, "I was in love with Joey, and he put me up to it. He told me he wanted Mary Jo out of the picture so that we could be together—but I'm sorry I ever believed him."

And there are constant reminders of her former lover and his wife thanks to continual TV and press coverage of the case even years after it happened.

"It makes me sick to see Mary Jo all lovey-dovey with him on the TV, holding his hand and standing by his side," Amy told one prison pal.

"I was with Joey all the time when I was working in his escort service. I had a lot of fun doing that—Joey always treated me great. I used to go by their house to see Joey, and Mary Jo and I had always gotten along real well."

Some time later Amy Fisher made a bizarre outburst about her notorious case when she watched a TV movie based on her case with another inmate inside Bedford Hills.

As Mary Jo Buttafuoco's face was shown after she'd been shot, Amy stood up and said, "Isn't that a beautiful sight," and then marched out of the television room.

There were many other examples of Amy's bizarre behavior inside Bedford Hills and Albion.

One time she bit off all her fingernails and gave them to another woman inmate as a gift.

"I thought it was sick," commented the prisoner later.

As Amy's sentence progressed she became increasingly infuriated by her incarceration. She threw tantrums and stomped and screamed hysterically because she felt others weren't paying enough attention to her.

During one incident, Amy got up in the middle of the night and threw a jug of Kool-Aid over a woman she'd had a feud with.

"She was always doing hateful things like that and trying to blame others," says one inmate. It seemed that Amy never really appreciated she was just another prisoner like every other woman in Albion.

"Even the prison guards treated her like she was a celebrity," says one inmate. "And she loved being in the spotlight all the time. She wanted nonstop attention. She hated it when everything died down and her name wasn't mentioned so much."

One inmate who enjoyed a sexual liaison with Amy Fisher provides a fascinating insight into life inside prison for two illicit lovers.

Elaine "Lizsette" San Miguel exchanged passionate love letters with Amy as well as having a highly charged physical relationship.

"We were attracted to each other right from the start," explains the 30-year-old strawberry blonde, who had already served nine years on a manslaughter charge when the Long Island Lolita arrived at Albion in December, 1992.

San Miguel related to Amy because she'd been imprisoned at a young age just like her. She called Amy "Kitten." Amy called her "Lizsette" or "Sammie."

Soon the two women found themselves embroiled in a passionate affair that was punctuated by Amy's letters, which were secretly slipped to her out of sight of prison guards.

Early on in the friendship, Amy made it very clear that she wanted to have sex with San Miguel.

My darling Lizsette,

You are the object of my desire, my obsession. I'm yearning to caress your toes

and gaze into your eyes. Please let me love
you.

Forever,
Kitten.

On paper ripped from a notebook—or occasionally on personalized stationery given to her
by her mother—Amy wrote about her hopes and
desires, her fears, and her loneliness. Amy even
decorated the notes with childlike drawings and
sealed them with candy-pink lipstick kisses.

Amy's true fears and trepidations about life in
prison sometimes came to the surface.

"In one letter she said she was frightened
she'd go mad," explains San Miguel. "She said
she'd been locked up like an animal, stuck behind bars while her friends outside were leading
productive, eventful lives."

But in another letter Amy seemed upbeat and
determined to survive. She even listed all the
things she wanted to do when she was released:

1. Travel the world in 80 days.

2. Have "wild sex" with Ronald Mc-
   Donald.

3. Model fur coats on Madison Avenue.

4. Have cosmetic surgery on her nose.

5. Have a baby.

6. Have her portrait painted in the nude.

7. Go topless sunbathing on the Riviera.

8. Get a tattoo.

I'd even like to hang around gay bars with you, Elaine. But only if you take me, wrote Amy.

Amy even told San Miguel, who says she's been gay since the age of 14, that she'd slept with a woman before jail—a hairstylist from Long Island.

"You're both beautiful," Amy told her new girlfriend, "and I love beautiful things." She also admitted to San Miguel she had sex with other girls in the jail before she met her.

One time, Amy was yet again in lockdown after refusing a work detail. She used that solitary confinement to pen yet another note to San Miguel.

Hi Sweetheart,

I wonder how long I'll be kept in here. The pain of not being able to see you is unbearable . . .

Amy went on to say she'd been using the time in solitary to go on a diet and to think up a name for "our" first child.

"*I hope it's [a] girl Lizsette.*"

When Amy got out of solitary the relationship between the two women continued and Amy would sneak into San Miguel's bed cubicle after everyone else had gone to sleep.

"We would kiss and play and hold each other," San Miguel admits.

Amy even tried to impress San Miguel by twistedly claiming she'd turned tricks for men from the age of 15.

"I loved it—I loved the money," she insisted.

Amy became so besotted with her secret lover that she wrote yet another letter:

Hello my beautiful,

Damn I love you. This isn't fair. You're so close yet it seems like you're a million miles away.

I know you don't think I'm gay, and you may be right. But I do know I love you with all my heart.

My feelings are genuine and I'm gonna keep telling you I love you until you believe it.

But gradually San Miguel's love for Amy cooled. The troubled teenager became distraught about the impending break-up. In a last bid to revive the relationship Amy even tried to make herself more sexually attractive to her lesbian friend.

"She had her mom and lawyer send her some beautiful things like Lancôme makeup, blouses, shoes, Victoria's Secret lingerie. Amy kept her room immaculately tidy and she tried to clean up her appalling language, too."

But San Miguel had already concluded that Amy was not a genuine lesbian and therefore the relationship was going nowhere.

"She used her body to get her way in everything—from turning tricks at 15 to snaring Joey Buttafuoco,'' recalls San Miguel.

San Miguel eventually got herself moved to another housing unit. But Amy followed two weeks later. "I still cared for her as a friend; but she wanted to have sex with me every minute of the day. She seemed completely shocked that I didn't want to be with her every second.''

By all accounts Amy was devastated. But she continued to pursue San Miguel. One time San Miguel stood up Amy after agreeing to meet. Amy was so devastated she wrote her lover a note.

Sam,

Why did you stand me up at the gym?

P.S. I made you pizza but when you didn't show up, I ate it. It was really good!

In desperation, Amy even tried to make San Miguel jealous by exposing her breasts to two other female inmates in the prison yard.

"I felt like smacking her,'' San Miguel recalls. "I just ended up walking away from her—I knew if I hit Amy they would have buried me under the jail because of who she was.''

When the topless incident failed, Amy made one last bid to re-ignite the romance:

How come you see nothing wrong with selling my body, but you see something wrong with me opening my shirt?

> I love you so much it hurts. And the other times I want to kill you.

San Miguel got herself transferred, this time back to the prison's L-Block to get away from Amy. During those months, the two women only saw each other in the prison beauty parlor where San Miguel worked. But still the letters kept pouring in. Although this time they were full of wounded pride:

> I'm not a sucker. You want respect, baby, earn it! Play fair.

But as their love faded so the real Amy Fisher emerged.

San Miguel says, "Like everyone else, I thought Amy was a sweet, innocent child because she was only 19—but I learned differently. She could turn it on or off and could become a real spoiled brat."

And Amy infuriated many inmates by her attitude. She even bragged in prison that she'd been offered a million dollars by *Playboy* to pose as a nude centerfold after she got out of jail.

Elaine San Miguel left on July 19, 1993; the pair never even had a chance to say goodbye. But some time later Amy Fisher wrote to her:

> Dear Liz,
>
> Honey, why are you acting like this? Won't you talk to me? Don't you care? I'm very confused so I'm going to end this now.

Peace and good luck. I love you—even though you don't believe it.

Soon Amy Fisher was on the lookout for a new companion.

In July 1994, while back at Albion Prison, she began a *Fatal Attraction*-type of obsession with another attractive fellow inmate. The two women had first met a few months earlier while both were attending a prison course on how to control anger.

The inmates had to do skits and sing. One time after the other inmate had sung, Fisher wrote her a note saying that her voice turned her on.

"I'm not in this course because I have any remorse. I'm here to watch you," she wrote.

Then Amy tried to ignite the affair by sending the other inmate a note, reading,

Before I leave I want to make love to you. I don't care when. I don't care how, all I know is I just have to.

The note concluded: *Love forever into the next eternity* and was signed, *Red Devil*.

The other inmate was serving a sentence for selling cocaine. In July 1994, Amy was moved into the other inmate's dormitory and given a job in the prison hospital where she worked as a nurse's aide.

Not long after this Amy moved alongside the other inmate and told her, "I want to watch every step you take."

The woman refused to talk to Amy. But then

Amy became extremely vindictive toward the object of her desires.

Amy made up a story that the other inmate had beaten her up. Four days later the woman was placed in solitary confinement at the prison's special housing unit.

When she got out after 75 days authorities reclassified her from medium security to maximum security and transferred her to Bedford Hills.

Prison documents show that the other woman was disciplined following her alleged attack on Amy Fisher, but they also show that the decision against that woman was later reversed without explanation.

The other inmate never succumbed to Amy Fisher's desires, but she claims she genuinely feared for her life when she rejected the younger woman.

"Amy was spittin' blood about bein' rejected by [her] and for a while we all thought she'd get cut," says one inmate.

In January, 1995, Amy Fisher's lawyer filed a claim against the Albion Correctional Facility indicating she planned to sue the state of New York for unspecified damages for failing to protect her from attacks from other inmates and staff.

"This is a horrific situation where the people who are in charge of the system are a lot worse than the people they are being paid to maintain," explained Fisher's lawyer David Brietbart.

Correctional officials emphatically denied the allegations, saying Amy had made the same charges before and was simply trying to pressure the state to move her to a prison closer to her family's Long Island home. They even claimed she had been upset when she was transferred from Bedford Hills to Albion more than 10 hours away from Long Island.

"We do not succumb to blackmail," said James Flateau, spokesman for the Department of Correctional Services. "Amy has a longstanding request to get closer to home and we have refused to do that because people get moved closer to home based on good behavior. Amy has a history of breaking the rules."

In the four-page legal document, Fisher claimed that she was "raped by a correctional officer employed at the Albion Correctional Facility while being escorted from her housing quarters."

The court papers also said that on September 23, 1994, Fisher was "violently attacked" by one or more inmates after warning prison officials that she needed protection.

Stories of further sexual abuse by guards later surfaced when Amy Fisher smuggled a diary out of prison in a desperate bid to let the outside world know that she had been twice raped.

The startling personal account spelled out in horrifying detail Amy Fisher's claims that she was sexually assaulted, forced to pose for nude photographs with another inmate and had her clothes urinated on by guards at the prison.

Prison officials even tossed her into solitary confinement for 60 days on charges she sexually harassed a prison guard.

Amy believed that authorities were trying to shut her up before she blew the lid off the shocking jailhouse sex scandal.

"They are complete animals," the tormented (now) 21-year-old wrote in her diaries. "I've been beaten down, raped, and verbally harassed and threatened on a daily basis. I've been going through hell for the last four years.

"The real reason I'm in lock (solitary) is because I was raped by an officer in April and I reported it. This is their way of trying to break me down."

Amy claimed she had been kept in solitary for months on end.

"I'm just scared because they roughed me up and urinated on my belongings. This place is a nightmare. They think because we are in jail that they can do and take what they want."

Amy said she was raped for the first time as she was being transported from housing quarters. Prison officials ignored her complaint, but she smuggled out her diary to her lawyer in a bid for justice. In it she wrote, "I have a pair of panties from when a corrections officer intimidated me into having sex with him."

Those panties were tested for traces of semen. There was even talk that a blood sample would be obtained from the officer in question to see if it matched. At the time of writing this still had not been done.

This is an account of another rape Amy Fisher says occurred at the prison in April, 1996:

A male officer called the unit where she lived

and said she had legal mail and to come and get it.

Amy went to see him in an office at about 3 P.M. and he told her he was busy and asked her to come back at 8 P.M. She went back and the same officer told her to have a seat and wait. Amy waited until 8:30. Then another woman inmate left the office.

The officer then re-emerged and beckoned her into his office.

"Have a seat," he told Amy.

"I just need my mail 'cause I gotta get back," replied Amy, according to her later testimony.

Then, she claimed, the officer began making sexual suggestions to her.

"You don't have any legal mail. I just wanted to see you alone," said the officer.

Amy claimed she then got up and tried the door. It was locked.

The officer grabbed Amy around the waist.

"You can make things easy for yourself . . . or hard," he told her.

Amy did exactly what he told her to do. She claimed he raped her in that office.

Following that alleged attack, Amy Fisher said she had further evidence of sexual abuse by guards.

"I have naked photos of myself and a friend of mine, which were taken by a guard," she wrote. "My friend and I stole some of the photos from him."

When she tried to go public with her claims she was once again put in solitary confinement.

"Prison is like a world with its own rules,"

she wrote. "They can do anything to you and you can't prove it."

According to Amy's attorney, women's prisons are a sexual candy store for the guards.

"It's a virtual whorehouse for the male guards. The women are abused and worse by many of the guards. Amy is treated worse because she is considered a celebrity," he said.

Amy Fisher's mother, Rose, has demanded fairer treatment for her daughter.

"The Department of Corrections' recent actions are obviously an attempt to cover their own backside, because they know my attorneys are going to go to court over the physical attacks on Amy," said her mother.

Meanwhile back once again behind the grim bars of Bedford Hills, Amy Fisher led an increasingly lonely life.

"We can have personal shirts, but only solid colors. We can't have my favorite colors, black and blue," said Amy, claiming her gay sex life is a thing of the past. "I don't dress up much, 'cause I refuse to look hot for a bunch of dykes. They swear they're gay and it's strange 'cause most of them have tons of kids—go figure."

But there is another almost childlike side to Amy that came across clearly in one of her longest diary entries:

"I don't cry a lot and people tell me I'm hard, but I learned not to expect a hell of a lot from human nature. I always seem to make the wrong choices romantically.

"I made up this list of people not to get involved with—married people, poor people, people over 35, and people with severe health problems. I figure as long as I follow the list, I'll save myself emotional headaches."

Undoubtedly, prison has hardened her attitude toward many things. "I like all types of music, depending on my mood," she writes. "I'm into eating healthy. I don't eat red meat. Once in a while maybe a cheeseburger, but that's it.

"Actually now that I think about it, I may not be so healthy, 'cause I absolutely love chocolate. It's my downfall. I weigh 95 pounds and I'm one of those short people, 5-feet-4.

"I have ugly feet, so I bless the person who invented socks. I am a smoker and have tried to quit a few times to no avail."

But, like so many inmates, Amy Fisher had mixed feelings about the future. (She should be out of prison by the time this book is published.) "I've started my one-year countdown till parole, but I'm also scared to death. I feel like I'll be lost and alone to start from scratch.

"I feel I won't be able to cross the street without holding someone's hand. This is what I agonize about at night."

Amy Fisher still claimed that lover Joey Buttafuoco brainwashed her into trying to kill his wife.

"It's ironic—I'm here and Buttafuoco is in Hollywood making movies. I'm just depressed and tired of being locked in this monkey cage," she wrote.

But Fisher felt genuine remorse about what happened to Buttafuoco's wife. "I am embarrassed by what I did and feel pretty bad about it, too. I was young and I've grown through all of this.

"I'm a deep person and don't want to think about some terrible stupid mistake I made when I was 17. I hope someday I can do something really great and people will ask me all about that instead."

Amy's complaints, especially about Albion Prison, were eventually superseded by an extraordinary scandal involving male guards spying on inmates stripping before showertime. Those male members of staff even later watched video recordings of those female inmates undergoing strip searches.

As the women removed their clothing, female guards filmed them with a hand-held camera while male guards watched through a partially open door, according to claims later filed by inmates at Albion.

Those prisoners claimed that the filming was just the latest in a long line of sexual harrassment, inflicted on inmates by male members of staff.

"They wanted to focus on what they wanted, and what they wanted was not to focus on the frisk by the officers, but on the women and their bodies."

Inmate Leonides Cruz told investigators, "There were two female officers taping, but the door was open a crack and two male officers were looking in."

She claims she was ordered to touch her own body and then her mouth in a suggestive manner.

"Then I had to bend over . . . in front of the camera—it was so embarrassing and humiliating. I wouldn't fight it because I knew that things would get worse for me. When they finished videotaping and I came out they were all laughing . . ."

Another inmate, Patti, was also subjected to the naked videotaping on her arrival at Albion.

"The sergeant escorted me in there—and I saw they had turned on the cameras. In the room there were two female officers standing in this dirty room, with a filthy floor.

"Two male officers were standing outside and I could see them looking in. The female officers started filming and asked me to strip—one piece of clothing at a time, like a striptease.

"I couldn't believe what was happening to me. After my clothes came off, they asked me to lift my breasts. Then they told me to turn around and bend over . . .

"I was so humiliated that I started to cry, and the officer laughed and said, 'Tears don't cut it here—you're in a real jail now.'"

Others claim that male and female officers routinely touched inmates' genitals and felt their breasts with the palms of their hands.

Some months later the prison's authorities offered each of the inmates $1,000 in compensation. "You can draw your own conclusions from that," says one Albion inmate.

THREE
Jean

FROM A WINDOW NEAR HER CELL, JEAN HARRIS used to watch as the seagulls circled Bedford Hills Correctional Facility after sailing over the 12-foot-high perimeter fence topped with razor wire. The birds would then gracefully swoop down on the prison's bleak yard.

As Jean Harris later recalled, "Watching those birds you suspected that if you didn't think you're a prisoner, then maybe you weren't one. The trick was just to keep looking up."

Jean served 12 years for shooting to death her lover—famous Scarsdale Diet author Herman Tarnower. She always maintained that the shooting of her lover Tarnower was an accident (she says she intended to kill herself, and the gun went off during the struggle).

It's all light-years away from the life she once led as headmistress of the exclusive Madeira School for Girls in McLean, Virginia.

But even Jean Harris conceded that prison is

a place where "good is bad and black is white and decency and truth are held laughable."

The atmosphere inside Bedford Hills can have a disturbing effect on the women inmates.

Jean spent the first 10 years of her sentence at Bedford "being an arrogant bitch" before she "finally got wise and kept my mouth shut."

While in Bedford, Jean spent six hours a day teaching parenting classes to the pregnant women and new mothers among the inmates as well as caring for the inmates in the prison nursery.

But despite all this Jean regularly suffered from bouts of frustration and despondency. She even had two heart attacks while in custody.

However, Jean—unlike many other inmates—was galvanized by what she had seen in prison; a woman and her infant dying from AIDS; another having the first of her 14 children when she was raped at the age of 10. And there were many more.

Yet despite her good work inside prison, she remained very aloof from most of the other inmates. "We've sort of gotten used to one another," she said in 1993. "Most of them have a lot of respect for their grandmothers, and I'm the closest thing to a grandmother around."

Jean lived on an honor floor—the prison's cleanest and brightest housing—at Bedford Hills but still found prison life extremely grim. After working most of the day in the nursery she would return to her cell to read her mail, a newspaper, magazines. Anything to break the tedium.

Jean Harris received thousands of letters following her conviction and in some ways they certainly helped her come to terms with her alleged crime.

Almost every evening at Bedford Hills, Jean dined with two other honor-floor inmates in the unit's rec room. They prepared their meals in a small kitchen shared by 30 to 50 women.

Usually they ate salads and afterwards would watch the MacNeil-Lehrer Newshour before the guard locked Jean into her cell early to read until she fell asleep. Reading provided her only true escape from prison.

But Jean Harris was no ordinary prisoner. She worked with a nun who founded the prison's parenting program for pregnant women inmates. She also wrote three books that she claimed "helped make people aware that women in prison have children and need to see those children and nurture them."

Jean also joined the prison authorities by advising other inmates not to waste the time they spend in prison, because it could be the last leisure time they have without responsibilities.

On her release on parole in March 1993, Jean Harris did not even experience the same job-hunting problems faced by most ex-cons.

Within weeks of gaining her liberty she landed work as a contributing editor to *Lear's*, the monthly magazine aimed at women over 40.

But as current Bedford Hills inmate Shenée Green points out, "The rest of us ain't so lucky. There ain't much future for us."

In the years of her incarceration at Bedford Hills, just 15 miles from the scene of the shooting, Jean Harris made many influential friends, including Barbara Walters and author Shana Alexander, who wrote *Very Much a Lady*, the 1983 book about the case.

A model prisoner, Harris was to prove to be her own best character witness.

"She [could] have gone to prison and moped and dug herself into a hole," says Harris's attorney Leon Friedman. "Instead, every day she woke up and said, 'What can I do constructive today?' That's the kind of person she is."

Harris was one of the lucky ones—she got out to see the crocuses bloom. Many don't.

FOUR
Precious

A HIGH-PROFILE PRISON LIKE BEDFORD HILLS has its fair share of media coverage. When the infamous women criminals arrive there is a flurry of news stories about them often followed up for many months by salacious tales in the tabloids.

But while those inmates undoubtedly spark interest and intrigue among the rest of the prison population, they eventually become fully integrated into jail society like everyone else.

However, every now and again an inmate gains notoriety long *after* being incarcerated.

Take Precious Bedell. She was serving 25-years-to-life for killing her 18-month-old daughter La Shonda in the toilet of a Syracuse restaurant in November, 1979, when she was just 24 years of age at the time. She faced incarceration knowing she had lost control and killed her own flesh and blood.

The District Attorney at that time was William Fitzpatrick. He recalls, ''Precious was in a restaurant and the child was being disruptive. She took her into the ladies' room. I don't recall whether the child had soiled her pants, but the daughter continued to be disruptive. Precious took her into a booth. What happened in there no one knows but Precious.

"The medical evidence was that the child's head was struck against a blunt object, probably a wall, while she was shaken in an effort to keep her quiet."

After her conviction for murder, Precious was moved to Bedford Hills where she has remained ever since. At first, like many other new inmates, she was aggressive and deeply disturbed by her predicament.

But eventually she started an education course and gained a degree, qualified as a prison library clerk, and became one of the most popular inmates at Bedford Hills.

"Precious has become like a mother figure to many of us. The younger women often turn to her when they're having problems in and out of the prison," says another inmate serving a life sentence.

Precious even organized a Parents As Reading Partners program for other inmates and served as chairwoman of the Inmate Foster Care Committee.

"The change in Precious was incredible. Here was this angry, bitter, heartbroken woman who'd killed her own child in a heat of the moment incident. She was torn up inside," says the other inmate. "But gradually she got her shit together and started to use her time in prison to educate and improve herself.''

For years Precious kept a low profile inside Bedford. And—unlike many—she never denied committing the crime she was accused of.

As fellow inmate Shenée Green explains, ''Everyone in here says they're innocent. It's the guilty ones that stand out. But it's the same most every place.''

Then Hollywood star Glenn Close got involved in the Precious case.

The actress first met Precious Bedell in 1991 when she visited Bedford Hills to research a movie role. The two women eventually formed a close bond of friendship, swapping letters almost every month. Close became a familiar visitor to the prison over the following few years.

Precious convinced Glenn Close she was a changed person. Close even told journalists she would trust Precious with her own daughter.

Close then began actively backing the growing campaign—orchestrated by Precious's own very determined efforts—to have the remainder of her sentence commuted.

During a court bid to re-examine the case, Close even wrote a letter to the judge explaining why she believed Precious should be released.

''She has become a role model for the women she teaches and counsels within her prison walls,'' said Close.

Precious even helped write a foster care handbook for jailed parents and at the time of this writing was completing a Master's degree in psychology so she could be of even more help to high-risk children.

Her foster care handbook was so highly praised across the country that it helped raise the profile of her own campaign for freedom.

"I would describe Precious as extraordinary. That pamphlet she has written to help young mothers under stress similar to hers will save children's lives," stated Glenn Close.

"She has served many years for an incident that lasted about eight seconds. If she were released now, justice would have been served."

Even the Bedford Hills' staff, plus lawyers and state officials have backed Precious's campaign for freedom. However that may not be enough.

In 1994, Precious appealed to then-New York Governor Mario Cuomo for her sentence to be reduced. She was turned down.

The courts themselves are powerless to set aside her sentence for murder in the second degree although a swell of public support may well influence the new state governor to grant her clemency.

Inmates at Bedford are continuing to encourage Precious to keep on fighting for her freedom.

"We told her to keep on battling. We know she'll get there in the end," says one of Precious's closest friends inside Bedford.

Meanwhile Precious continues helping the needy and disturbed souls of Bedford in a selfless, humane way. She proves that sometimes—albeit rarely—out of a long prison sentence some good can be achieved.

FIVE

Pam

PAM SMART'S CASE MADE MANY HEADLINES
around the world, especially when sexy pictures
of her surfaced, stripped down to skimpy bra and
panties for kinky romps with her teenage lover.
Bedford Hills inmate Pam also became the subject of a TV film starring Helen Hunt and the
inspiration for the hit Nicole Kidman movie *To
Die For*. It was certainly a crime that will not be
easily forgotten

Winnacunnet High School nestled on the edge of
the quiet New England town of Hampton and
enjoyed a reputation as one of the finest schools
in the state. None of those educational problems
of truancy and violence existed here. It was actually a pleasant environment where people were
at peace with themselves. Or so it seemed.

The white wood detached homes that domi-
nated the area with their neatly trimmed front
lawns were classic evidence of the harmony. It

was a small, tightly knit community that enjoyed an influx of vacationers in the summer months but still managed to remain a crime and scandal-free community.

In the classrooms of Winnacunnet High a strict moral code was abided by to the letter. Anyone who stepped out of line could expect severe punishment. There were few rebels among the school ranks. although Bill Flynn, Patrick Randall, and Vance Lattime definitely tried to fit into that category.

They were even called ''The Three Musketeers'' by other pupils and staff. It marked them apart and made their own feeling of isolation from the school's mainstream society more complete.

Bill Flynn was the self-appointed leader of the Musketeers despite looking even younger than 15.

In the schoolyard the boys would comment on girls from a distance. But in reality none of them had the courage of their convictions. They were all virgins.

The Three Musketeers didn't like admitting it to themselves—let alone their contemporaries. They even tried to convince their pals that they were actually very experienced with girls.

So perhaps it was surprising when Bill agreed to attend a self-esteem class for teenagers run by a member of the school staff called Pamela Smart. She was 20 years old with long legs and pretty, streaked blonde hair.

Musketeer Bill couldn't take his eyes off her

from the moment he walked into her self-esteem class one November evening. He gazed longingly at the contours of her breasts beneath her tight-fitting sweater. Then he noticed her wedding ring and presumed that the furthest he would get with sexy Pam was as a fantasy figure in his memory bank.

But not long after starting the self-esteem classes, a strange thing happened. Bill and his Musketeers were hanging around the schoolyard when Pam Smart brazenly approached him.

"Will you come to my office after school, Billy? It's important," she gushed at the teenager before walking off in the direction of the staff coffee room.

Patrick and Vance were impressed.

"Hey, Billy. She wants you man!"

They'd picked up on the way she called him "Billy."

Bill was actually deeply embarrassed and rather bewildered by Pam Smart's approach. He presumed she wanted to discuss some school work.

Pam Smart's office at Winnacunnet High School was not particularly impressive. It consisted of a table and two chairs plus shelves crammed with schoolbooks.

She only had the office because—besides being media studies teacher at the school—she also had to write up all the school's press releases for distribution to the local newspapers and TV stations.

In the evenings Pam also worked as a DJ on

a local hard rock station. She loved the loudest, most raucous bands like Van Halen, Led Zeppelin, and Deep Purple.

The staff at the radio station greatly appreciated Pam because of her penchant for wearing extremely sexy outfits ranging from skintight stone-washed jeans to black leather mini-skirts.

But that sexy image was complemented by a softer, more charitable side when she volunteered to run the self-esteem class for the many hapless Winnacunnet High teenagers who needed the sort of guidance she was more than happy to provide.

But then Pam knew only too well how difficult those teenage years could be. She actually got a real buzz out of helping the kids to discover some much-needed self-esteem.

On a personal level the previous few months of Pam's life had been a period of great upheaval. That May she had married her college sweetheart, Greg. They had moved into a comfortable apartment in the nearby community of Derry, New Hampshire.

Greg's work as a salesman meant he spent much of the week away from home, and Pam did not like spending so many lonely nights at home, often with only her dog for company. That was another reason why she volunteered to run the self-esteem classes and turned up as a regular DJ on the local radio station.

Pam also quite enjoyed the attention of the teenage boys who turned up at her self-esteem classes.

She noticed Bill Flynn's attentive gaze. But

then Pam had enjoyed being a flirt since her early teens, and getting married did nothing to curtail the habits of a lifetime.

She thought Bill was a good-looking boy. He had nice dark wavy hair and sea-blue eyes.

So when Bill turned up at Pam's office at the school as she had instructed him to do earlier, there was an air of apprehension about the proceedings.

Bill remained puzzled as to why he'd been asked to Pam's office.

Within seconds of arriving, she handed him an envelope. He did not question her actions. Instead he just took it and opened it.

"I hope you like them," was all Pam said as the teenager nervously ripped open the envelope.

He couldn't quite believe what he found. They looked like family snapshots. Bill was confused. Was she showing her pictures of her family?

"Go on. Go ahead and look," urged Pam.

Bill still hesitated. None of it made any sense.

"Go on. Have a look," she repeated.

As he took the photos out of the envelope he froze. His eyes locked onto one particular shot. Then another and another.

They all showed her in skimpy underwear kneeling on a bed, pouting her lips in a "come here now" sort of way. She had a glint in her eyes. She looked as if she was about to have sex.

Her body was sensational. Bill's hands were shaking. He was bewildered.

Here was 15-year-old Bill Flynn sitting in a teacher's office while she showed him near-nude photographs of herself. His pals would never believe him when he told them.

Pam Smart was watching her nervous young pupil for his reactions. She could see that he couldn't take his eyes off her body.

Pam got up and walked around to the side of the desk where Bill was sitting. He was still clutching the photos in his increasingly sweaty hands.

Pam leaned against the desk and started quietly singing the words from her favorite Van Halen song "Hot For Teacher." It was all about the seduction of a pupil by his teacher. Bill dropped the photos on the desk.

Pam then stroked Bill's hair gently. She picked up the snapshots from the desk and handed them back to Bill. "Find the one you like best."

Pam liked looking at those photos herself because it made her feel sexy. When she'd posed for the pictures while her best friend Tracey Collins snapped away, she kept urging her to make sure they looked really hot. "Do you think they're sexy enough? Tell me they are. Tell me they are."

The photos had originally been intended to turn on husband Greg. But he was appalled when Pam showed them to him and demanded that she destroy them immediately. Greg was no fun. She decided to find someone else who would appreciate the photos.

Back in the office with young Bill still staring at the photos, Pam heard a noise outside the office. She pulled her hand away from Bill's and whispered, "Don't worry. You'll have me next time."

Bill Flynn was baffled. Had she really shown him those photos? Was she really coming on to him? Was he really going to sleep with her?

Bill couldn't get Pam out of his mind. She represented the best opportunity he'd ever had to lose his virginity.

And it wasn't just a sexual thing either. Young Bill thought he might be falling in love for the first time. He decided not to tell the other Musketeers about what had happened in Pam's office.

The day after that incident, Bill bumped into Pam in a school corridor. She touched his arm softly and said, "Come to my home tonight." Then she gave him a scrap of paper with her address. Bill was ecstatic. Was all this really happening?

Pam Smart had been planning this moment in her mind for quite some time. She wanted—and needed—someone to comfort her, make love to her. Someone who would be there when Greg was not.

Marriage to Greg had seemed a great idea initially. They'd first met as teenagers and enjoyed a mutual love of hard rock, leather jackets, and a fun lifestyle.

But then Greg got himself a "serious" job as an insurance salesman. He wanted to grow up, have a family, take his life more seriously. But Pam was still young and carefree and determined to stay that way.

She'd kept the part-time job as a DJ because she did not want to let go of that lifestyle.

Just a few weeks before that encounter with Bill, Pam and Greg had a huge fight when Greg announced he was going skiing with some friends. Pam couldn't understand why he wanted to leave her alone when he was already often away from home for work.

That night Pam told her husband she wished she'd never married him.

Greg was very hurt by the remark and retaliated in a crushing outburst that included a confession that he'd had a one-night stand while working away from home a few weeks previously. He excused it by claiming he was drunk at the time.

Pam was mortified. It was the ultimate betrayal.

From that day on a gnawing hatred for Greg began to grow inside Pam.

Now she was about to welcome a 15-year-old virgin pupil to her home so she could exact revenge on her husband.

Pam had planned it all with great precision. She'd even rented *9 ½ Weeks* on video. Pam had watched it before with husband Greg and she'd been really turned on by it. Her icebox was filled to the brim with beers to guarantee the teenager would feel completely in the mood.

The stage was set.

Bill Flynn was feeling extremely nervous in the hours before he was due to call at Pam's apartment. He'd never had sex before and some perfectly reasonable fears began to run through his mind.

By the time he actually got to her home, he was wishing he'd never gone there. He wanted to turn around and go home. He feared that Pam thought he was sexually experienced. In fact she was only too well aware of his limitations and that was what turned her on. She wanted the power to decide where and when it would happen.

Bill forced himself to press the doorbell. The moment Pam answered he felt he'd done the right thing. She looked brilliant. Her lips were glossed and full. Her hair cascaded onto her shoulders. Her tight skirt was high above the knee. Her skin-tone pantyhose looked silky smooth. There was even a hint of her bra through the opened top three buttons of her blouse.

Then as he walked in, Bill noticed one of Pam's friends sitting on the couch. He was very disappointed.

He awkwardly introduced himself to Pam's friend Cecilia Pierce. Pam got Bill a beer and they settled in front of the TV to watch *9 ½ Weeks*.

Bill actually felt a tad uncomfortable watching all that sex on the small screen. But what he didn't realize was that this was all part of Pam's carefully scripted plan.

Earlier that day she had informed her friend Cecilia she was inviting her teenage pupil to the apartment. She made it clear she planned to seduce him. But she wanted Cecilia to pretend to be Bill's girlfriend in case anyone called round at the apartment. Ironically Cecilia was nearer to Bill's age—she was just 16.

As the end credits for the movie rolled, Pam got up and went into the kitchen. Cecilia smiled knowingly.

Bill was at a loss for words. He was confused. Where exactly did Cecilia fit in?

Just then Pam reappeared and offered to show Bill the rest of the apartment.

Her seduction of Bill Flynn was slow and deliberate. She was calling all the shots, naturally.

Cecilia departed soon afterwards and as she walked past the bedroom to the front door she saw a glimpse of two naked bodies entwined. The stereo was blaring out Van Halen's ''Hot For Teacher.'' It was an image she would never forget.

For the following few days Bill felt a twinge of guilt over what happened with Pam Smart. He could not quite believe he'd actually had sex with her and at the same time he felt emotionally drawn to her. It was a confusing mix of feelings for a 15-year-old boy to handle.

But Pam soon snapped him out of his confusion. Whenever they snatched a few moments together at the school she told him she wanted him. She even shed a few tears during one secret meeting in her office.

Over the following few weeks she began to suggest they could have a life together. Bill was scared *and* excited. Of course he knew she was married but maybe she'd give it all up for him?

Then one day she pulled him aside and told

him that there was something they had to do if they were going to get really serious.

"We've got to get rid of Greg. It's the only way."

Bill was reeling. What did she mean?

She made no attempt to elaborate and the subject was dropped.

A few days later Bill and Pam were making hot, steamy love in her car when she stopped in the middle of all the passion.

"Billy. If you really love me . . ."

She repeated her suggestion that he would have to get rid of Greg. Bill felt a great pull toward Pam, but why was she trying to make him do such a thing?

"Make it look like a break-in . . . Steal a few things from the bedroom . . . there's jewelry in there . . . the cops'll think Greg walked in . . . It's so simple."

Bill looked scared as she spoke. Then Pam summed up the priorities in her life.

"And don't do it in front of the dog. I don't want him scared."

Bill's dilemma was complete. He wanted nonstop sex. He wanted a relationship. But did he have to kill to prove it? After yet more insatiable lust he decided to do what she'd asked. He didn't quite know why but he felt he had to do it to keep her.

Bill recruited his two other Musketeers, Vance Lattime and Patrick Randall, to carry out the coldblooded murder of Greg Smart.

Pam had allowed him to bring the other two

into the plan because she knew that Bill wouldn't have the courage to do it alone.

All three teenagers remained hesitant about it at first and then convinced themselves it was "pretty cool." They actually considered that the $4,000 each they were going to make for the hit thanks to a life insurance policy on Greg was sufficient.

Pam had also persuaded them that it would be an easy plan to execute. They would steal a gun from Vance's father's vast collection of weapons. Pam even pointed out that if Greg wasn't killed outright they wouldn't make a penny. It *had* to work.

One night, with their friend Ray Fowler at the wheel, they raced up the freeway to Derry to carry out the killing. They were nervous but pumped up on adrenaline.

However, minutes before he got to the Smarts' apartment Bill got a twinge of conscience. He ordered Ray to turn the car around.

Thirty minutes later he met up with Pam and explained to her why the murder plan had not been carried through.

"We got kinda lost. I couldn't remember the street where you lived."

It was a feeble excuse from Bill and he knew it.

Pam was spitting blood.

"You don't love me. You got lost on purpose," she screamed at Bill.

He was frightened she was going to finish their relationship.

Pam then changed tactics. She began stroking

Bill's neck even though the other boys were standing next to them. She then led Bill towards her car and told the other boys to get lost.

Within seconds they were making love. Pamela was determined not to lose him yet. There was work to be done.

After hours of sex, she lay next to him and began to talk him through the murder of her husband.

"You've got to try again. This time make it work. If you don't, we shall have to stop seeing each other."

Bill agreed. He should have known better.

When the Three Musketeers burst into the Smart apartment as Greg was tidying up before his wife's return from work they didn't waste their words. Bill pointed Lance's father's gun at his lover's husband. His eyes darted to the wedding band. It had a special significance to Bill.

"Give us that ring, scumbag," he bellowed at the terrified Greg.

"If I gave it to you, my wife would kill me," said Greg. One of the other Musketeers snickered.

"Just give it to us."

But Greg was adamant. He'd just signed his own death warrant.

"Down on your knees!" yelled Bill.

He pointed the gun at the back of Greg's head and uttered three simple words, "God forgive me."

Greg Smart fell to the floor a split-second after the bullet entered his skull.

The Three Musketeers beat a hasty retreat.

* * *

At Greg's funeral a few weeks later, Pam Smart looked stunning dressed all in black. Head down, she tried to seem heartbroken.

As the priest referred to Greg's tragic death at the hands of unknown assailants, Pam shed a tear and dropped a bouquet of red roses onto the casket before it was covered with earth.

"God rest his soul . . ."

The Three Musketeers were, quite frankly, terrified. The newspaper headlines had made them realize the enormity of their deadly deed. And they still hadn't got any of their money from Pam.

She'd told them to stay away until she gave them the all-clear.

However, as the weeks progressed, the boys became more proud of what they had done. They even began bragging at school. Word started to get out.

"He was worth more dead than alive," boasted Patrick Randall to one classmate.

Only one of the Musketeers, Vance Lattime, was not so happy. He was having nightmares in which he kept seeing the face of Greg Smart over and over again.

His guilt would not go away. He began to question the entire scheme.

Vance's parents thought his introverted behavior was linked to girl problems. If only they'd realized who the girl was.

Then one day at breakfast Vance snapped. He broke down in tears and confessed to everything.

His parents were stunned. They went straight to the police.

In Derry, the news of the arrest of the Three Musketeers and their driver was taken extremely calmly by Pam Smart. She even told her 16-year-old friend Cecilia, ''Who are they going to believe? A 16-year-old or me with my professional reputation? I'll get off, don't worry. I'm never going to admit to the affair.''

Unluckily for Pam she did not notice the electronic tape recorder that was strapped to Cecilia's back.

On March 22, 1991, at a court in Exeter, New Hampshire, Pam Smart was found guilty of masterminding her husband's murder. She was sentenced to life imprisonment without the possibility of parole.

Bill Flynn, Patrick Randall, and Vance Lattime all admitted killing Greg Smart. Their life sentences were reduced to 28 years in exchange for their cooperation in helping the prosecution of Pamela Smart.

Inside Bedford Hills Pam is a tracker—a prisoner brought in from another state because her notoriety had made it difficult for her to get secure enough conditions in a prison nearer her home in New Hampshire.

Pam—inmate number 93G0356—was one of a handful of inmates accepted under an obscure legality, the Interstate Corrections Compact, which allows a state to transfer an inmate to another state for security reasons.

The state of New Hampshire was convinced that Pam needed a maximum security prison because she was a very high-profile inmate and they only had a medium-security facility for women.

Even before her trial had ended there had been numerous threats against Pam from "people telling us that they were going to take a dump truck and drive it over the fence around the yard or take a helicopter to rescue her when she was in the prison yard," explains one New Hampshire prisons official.

Under the Interstate Corrections Compact, prisoners had no say in when and where they were being transferred. As one court official puts it: "Just as an inmate has no justifiable expectation that he will be incarcerated in any prison within any state, he has no justifiable expectation that he will be housed in any particular state."

Pam's transfer occurred at 5:05 A.M. on March 11, 1993, when she was woken in her New Hampshire cell by the prison superintendent and told to pack her things.

As she admitted soon afterward, "It always loomed over my head that I would be moved to another prison." Her parents only found out through the television news.

Pam was the only person in New York State serving a sentence of life without parole (no such sentence exists under New York law).

Pam was also considered a flight risk and classified as a central monitoring case. This meant that she was under much higher security than most other inmates and had to be escorted whenever she moved between different units in the jail.

Pam almost immediately filed suit against the New York State Department of Corrections arguing that she was being unfairly classified as a "tracker." There are 10 such inmates at Bedford Hills.

"Nobody knew who I was when I got here," Smart said. "I was already a freak show in New Hampshire, but at Bedford people started asking who the new tracker was, and what she was in for."

Being housed in another state made it difficult for her family to visit, but her biggest concern was the appeals process. Before being moved she was able to see her lawyers once a week. On arrival at Bedford Hills it changed to once a month.

Her eventual appeal to the New Hampshire Supreme Court contended that she did not receive a fair trial. It was turned down and the Supreme Court of the United States refused to hear the case. At the time of this writing she had once again filed an appeal in the United States Court of Appeals in Concord, New Hampshire. One of the main points of her appeal was that she received an unfair trial because of the media attention.

Pam's mother, Linda Wojas, is also playing a major part in trying to get a new trial for her daughter. She even started an organization called Friends of Pam Smart, which does fund-raising to help pay her legal expenses.

"The reason she was transferred was because

we were very outspoken about my daughter's trial,'' said Ms. Wojas. ''She was tried and convicted in a twentieth century witch-hunt.''

Pam's mother and her group even lobby the state and federal government on her behalf. Ms. Wojas has appeared on more than 20 television interviews and held prayer vigils outside the prison gates in Goffstown, N.H., during the trial. Pam claims to get 60 letters of support each week.

Pam doesn't simply want a transfer back to New Hampshire. She has actually settled at Bedford Hills where she works as a teacher, studying criminal justice through a special prison correspondence program with the University of Alabama. Smart is also a member of the Long Termers Groups, a self-help group of inmates serving a minimum of 25 years.

Pam said: ''Because of my day-to-day life, I would prefer to stay here. There is more to do for my sanity here; it's not that I like it here.''

Pam Smart had already been nicknamed The Ice Maiden before she arrived at Bedford because of her lack of emotion throughout her incredibly high-profile trial.

But in Bedford, Pam turned her attention to other matters because of her own insatiable appetite for sex. She has regular secret trysts with her female lover. There have even been wild, violent brawls involving Smart and a number of other lesbian couples.

''Pam is insatiable. She openly boasts about her sexual appetite. We call women like her animals because they fuck whenever they feel like it with whoever takes their fancy,'' says one inmate who has been intimate with Smart.

With her once-slinky blonde hair now back to its original brunette color, Smart seems to many other inmates to be a very strong, dominating force inside Bedford Hills.

Pam has scrapbooks filled with newspaper clippings of her headline-hitting crime and subsequent conviction.

She lives in a two-story housing unit of single-occupancy cells for 120 women. Her 8-by-15-foot cell includes a toilet, sink, and bed.

Pam has put up her own patterned curtains in her cell and she also keeps a photo of her murdered husband on the wall. She continues to insist she's innocent.

''Pam feeds off her notoriety and believes that it makes her irresistible to the lesbian and bisexual women inside here,'' says one inmate.

Shortly after her incarceration, Pam started a relationship with a woman in jail on burglary and drug charges. She was 5' 10'' and weighed 200 pounds and, according to other inmates, ''very masculine.''

Pam and her illicit lover enjoyed regular sex in the bathroom of the prison's old school building. But the relationship soon developed into something more twisted.

''They made kinky, strap-on sex toys by wrapping an ace bandage tightly around a wad of napkins, pulling a rubber glove down tight over the top, and using the excess bandage ends to tie it around the waist,'' says one Bedford Hills source.

"And even though Pam's girlfriend was the masculine one in the relationship, she often insisted on playing the male role. It was typical Pam: pretty, cute, manipulative, even with a bull dyke who could have given her a severe beating if she got upset."

Being a tracker whose every move is supposed to be monitored within the prison, Pam should have been prevented from having her illicit sex sessions. But Pam's prison job as a teacher's aide meant she was able to move freely around the prison in the mornings.

"Pam is looked up to by many of the inmates and staff because of her middle-class background, and she takes full advantage of that," says one inmate at Bedford Hills.

Sources inside the prison claim that Pam has even had secret sex sessions with women staff members as well as numerous other inmates since her incarceration.

"Pam is into sex with anyone. She wants satisfaction. Inside prison there are always a few women like that. Sex is like a drug to them and as long as they get a regular fix they are reasonably content."

Intriguingly, Pam has made it clear she is not sexually interested in the male guards.

"They don't like her and she's too clever to get caught trying to seduce one of them 'cause then she'd have her privileges taken away," explains one inmate.

But over the years Pam has been getting a lot of unwanted attention from some female inmates with whom she has become bitter enemies. The feuds tend to be over sexual conquests.

The other inmates have even in some instances informed on Pam to get her locked down.

''Pam doesn't realize that some women look on their lovers as possessions and if another inmate moves in sexually on a woman then that can turn into a real heavy problem,'' explains one Bedford inmate.

Pam got her own back by snitching on other undiscovered couples by writing letters to the prison superintendent.

''Pam has been catching heat from a lot of girls because of her letters,'' says another prison inmate.

On October 28, 1996, one of those couples got revenge on Pam Smart.

While Pam was taking a smoking break one morning outside the prison's school building she was jumped by the two women.

The feminine partner got on Pam's back, while the masculine partner punched Pam flush in the face. Others saw what was happening but did nothing.

''As they started kicking Pam she tried to get up and one of them ripped her T-shirt off, exposing her breasts,'' says another inmate. ''One of them then grabbed her nipples and dug her nails in hard. They were screaming like wildcats.''

Eventually guards were alerted to the fight and the other two women were dragged off Pam. She was then covered in a blanket and escorted to the prison infirmary where they discovered that she had a fractured left eye socket.

Being a so-called celebrity inmate cuts no ice inside the caged heat of Bedford Hills.

PART TWO

The Cottage at Dwight Correctional Center, Dwight, Illinois

THERE IS AN EFFECTIVE AIR CONDITIONING SYStem in The Cottage and despite the scorching Illinois summers, heat is never as big a problem there as it is in the main penitentiary. Silver-gray metal fans turn rapidly in all the cells, circulating the cool air back and forth to give the place a calm atmosphere. The two-story structure's design effectively allows a cool rush of air to run through the premises throughout those scorching summer months.

It is a stone-built property, sitting like a vast sponge-colored cake among lush green fields in the prison grounds. The rooms are reasonably spacious, but stand side-by-side like a giant honeycomb within this sedate building. There is a hallway running between the rooms on each of the two main floors. Unlike most penitentiaries you cannot look up to rows of cells. This place is cozy, encapsulated, almost civilized.

On many afternoons the sun filters through the building's cathedral-size windows, casting a pleasant orange glow on the off-white walls. Some inmates complain about the blandness of the place, but it is a lot more cozy than most prisons and certainly less claustrophobic.

From the start, The Cottage was designed to alleviate the pressure of incarceration, and when you walk along the curling, gravelled path that leads to the thick oak front door, you suddenly understand why it is such a unique place. While Dwight's main penitentiary nearby dominates the horizon on the Illinois flatlands, this building is barely noticeable. It hangs in the shadow of the huge prison like some ineffective outhouse. Yet just 100 yards in front of it, thick barbed wire fencing twists ominously across the grassy fields.

Inside The Cottage, female eyes peer inquisitively out from the ground-floor windows as any stranger approaches. In the yard surrounding the building carefully nurtured rose bushes sprout neatly from the earth. This is not what one expects to find nestling in the grounds of a high-security prison.

The Illinois Bureau of Prisons has never before allowed a writer access to The Cottage, within the grounds of the Dwight Correctional Center, 80 miles south of Chicago, in the heart of Middle America. Most journalists only flock to a penitentiary when there is trouble; a riot; an execution; a well-publicized femme fatale. I had a different agenda.

Twenty-eight so-called hardened female criminals co-existed in The Cottage which looked more like an English country cottage than a section of one of America's toughest prisons. Only one *male* guard prevented them from escaping.

Ten years ago, prison authorities constructed the house away from the main prison building to hold up to 30 well-behaved long-term inmates. At first, a number of incidents of violence occurred, but as the authorities and inmates became more accustomed to the freedom offered by The Cottage, they began to appreciate its remarkable air of normality.

Prison staff say the main reason why The Cottage exists is because women criminals are not as prone to violence as men following incarceration. Men in nearby prisons claim it is sexual discrimination in reverse.

In recent years, The Cottage has contained inmates from a wide range of social backgrounds. There is also a roller-coaster ride of inmates' emotions from hatred to sorrow to humor and tragedy.

The Cottage is supposed to give so-called hardened women criminals a chance to prove they can look after themselves.

"It's got a good atmosphere compared with the prison. We all get on and do our thing without any hassle," says one inmate.

And the Dwight Correctional Center has other unique features as well.

In the summer of 1988 Dwight staff even introduced an onsite camping program so that inmates could spend some time with their children.

The program required minimal security staff

and was unaffected by the prison's crowded conditions and, most importantly, it offered great benefits to the inmates and their children.

Dwight—the only institution for women in the state of Illinois—managed to get a three-year federal grant to kick-start the scheme, known as the Camp Celebration. It is located in a large oak grove near the prison's main administration building. The site contains enough space for food and preparation storage areas, a large pavilion, and shower facilities.

The federal grant provided funding to build an equipment shed, buy camping and recreational supplies, and hire additional staff to administer the camp.

From 1991 the camp became self-sufficient and it runs for 13 weekends each summer, allowing up to 12 mothers per weekend to bring their children on grounds for a 48-hour visit.

A full-time camp director was hired, along with two interns, to oversee activities and make sure the program operated smoothly. Campmates—inmates assigned to help with the camp—handled food preparation, game check-out, animal care, and campground maintenance.

All women inmates are allowed to use the camp except those who are transferred, released, or unable to get their children to the camp. Also the warden has the right to refuse to allow a specific inmate to participate, especially if they have a history of violent child abuse or smuggling contraband into the facility.

A typical weekend camp is as follows:

* * *

FRIDAY: Children begin arriving around noon. They go through the prison security check at the main gate, their luggage is held for a more thorough search and returned to them by late afternoon.

Then each family receives camping equipment including sleeping bags, plastic moisture barrier sleeping pads, a cooler, a lantern, a cookstove and water jugs. Each campsite contains a four-person tent, a picnic table, and a trash can.

That afternoon children and parents get to know the others on site as facility staff prepare the Friday dinner at barbecue grills. It's typical camping food—hot dogs, hamburgers, ribs, and baked beans.

After dinner there are more games and families settle around the campfire singing. This usually winds up about nine allowing for showers and family time in the tents.

SATURDAY: Typical activities include pony rides, a mini-water slide, volleyball, badminton, board games, and arts and crafts.

An unusual feature of the camp is the farm animals supplied by nearby residents. These include—besides the pony—a lamb, goats, rabbits, and other animals, which are kept at the camp during the summer months and taken care of by the inmates.

The big event that night is the Family Skit Night where family members showcase their talents as a group or individually in skits, musical numbers, or pantomimes. The skits are followed by the central bonfire, with s'mores and roasted marshmallows as campfire treats, and a singalong that usually lasts about an hour. Families then take showers and head for their beds.

SUNDAY: Morning starts with a home-cooked breakfast of eggs, bacon, juice, and milk. Each mother cooks over the campstove for her children at their tent and is responsible for all preparation and cleanup. For some women, this is the first time in many years they have cooked breakfast for their children and for the majority it is their first experience with a campstove.

Inside Dwight the inmates who used the camp wrote down their feelings about the scheme.

One says, ''It allowed me to re-establish the mother-child relationship with my children. They could also ask me things without other family members or prison staff being present. I got the time to reassure my children that I loved them very much.''

Another comments, ''That program means so much to me. The best part of the project was the campfire. My children had never been camping before and the light of the campfire made them glow and toasting marshmallows made them giddy.''

Another says, ''My son had been living with his father for seven years and this was the first time I'd had him to myself in all that time. It was like getting to know him all over again. We played ball, but the main thing was there was no color barrier at all. That is what a lot of women have trouble with, but it didn't exist that weekend. We didn't notice nothing except the fun and joy of giving and sharing among ourselves.''

And finally: ''It's the best thing that's ever happened to me inside here. It was so good to be with my daughter and lie next to her. We talked about the day I'll return home and what it would feel like. If it feels a little like the camp did then I know it's what heaven will be like.''

However it must never be forgotten that Dwight is a high-security prison housing some of the most dangerous women in the nation.

SIX

Kathy

KATHY GAULTNEY, DRESSED IN A BLUE sweater, prison-issue white pants, sits on her bed in her cell. The walls are a putrid shade of yellow, the floor is bare tiles, and in the corner is a toilet. Two cardboard boxes contain her possessions—a frosted pink lipstick, a sweater, some law books, a diet drink.

Kathy gets up, sits at a school desk, then returns to the bed. This is her life now, shifting restlessly in her cell in The Cottage at the Dwight Correctional Facility for virtually half the day.

There is plenty of time to think about the incident that brought her here . . . and the appeal that might one day get her out.

The cliché that you never know what lies ahead of you certainly applies to the rotund grandmotherly figure of Kathy Gaultney.

She was a mother, a hardworking homemaker: happy, caring, loyal and content . . . everything, in short, that a wife in Middle America should be.

"I enjoyed bringing up the kids, seeing my friends in town for coffee, going on regular vacations. I'd never been in any trouble. I was just so ordinary. I was a good cook and my kids really seemed to appreciate me," says Kathy.

But then she got lured into a lifestyle that careered out of control.

St. Jacob is the sort of place where nothing much happens. A sleepy little hamlet set in the heart of the Illinois flatlands. The population of this tiny community is just 800 and the locals have always said that they dread the day it tops the 1,000 mark.

As you drive into St. Jacob you cannot help noticing the fertile fields that surround it on all four sides. Beautiful green pastures expertly farmed for maximum potential. They represent the real reason why the village even exists. Farming the land is the way most of the population lives and breeds—and that's the way they all want to keep it.

There are only a handful of streets in St. Jacob and they are never overflowing with traffic. A few pickup trucks and the occasional car rumble by—and everyone knows the owner of each automobile.

Perhaps not surprisingly, property prices in St. Jacob have never been high. You could pick up a perfectly reasonable detached home on the edge of town for 30,000 dollars—hardly a king's ransom by anyone's standards.

That was how Kathy Gaultney and her husband Keith came to settle in the town in the early 1980s. They had lived in some of the nearby larger communities over the years, but both of them fell in love with the peace and quiet of St. Jacob—and the house prices.

The problem was that neither Keith nor Kathy were working full-time. He organized construction site labor all over the state. But that meant months of solid work followed by long periods of inactivity. Kathy—who had just given birth to their son Walter—was the homemaker. The Gaultneys struggled to survive. But at least they had their pretty little white wooden-slatted cottage in St. Jacob—even though the modest mortgage repayments were proving very difficult to keep up.

Kathy Gaultney eventually got a job working behind the bar at a spit 'n' sawdust hostelry in nearby Collinsville. It wasn't well-paid but it kept the wolf from the door for the time being.

Back at home, Keith's own work was ominously slowing down and he'd taken to the bottle. Kathy ended up working all hours while Keith knocked back more and more booze. Most nights he'd collapse in a heap on their bed before Kathy even got home from her gruelling job at the tavern.

Kathy bit her lip and said nothing to her husband about his drinking. She convinced herself things would pick up and he'd sort himself out. But Keith Gaultney was on a downward spiral. His pride had taken a huge knock and he was sinking into alcoholic oblivion. He didn't really care any more. Just so long as Kathy kept working they could just about survive—and that would do him just fine.

One night in the bar where Kathy Gaultney worked she met a woman called Mary O'Guinn. By this time Kathy was very worried about Keith as the mortgage had not been paid for three months. She could barely afford to clothe her baby son and 11-year-old daughter Rachel from an earlier marriage. Kathy was not bashful about admitting her problems to anyone who would listen. She told Mary O'Guinn that she desperately needed to find a better-paying job.

O'Guinn—an attractive redhead—then made Kathy an offer she could not really refuse. It sounded like the opportunity of a lifetime. She told Kathy that she wanted her and her friend Martha Young to take over the New Way Toning Salon for housewives, in Collinsville. They could buy it with a loan from O'Guinn, who needed the office space behind the gym for her own business interests.

In that office O'Guinn planned to keep an assortment of weighing machines that had nothing to do with keeping people fit. These were small scales for weighing drugs before distributing them to a network of suppliers throughout the Midwest. Kathy Gaultney was about to become partner with one of the country's biggest drug cartels.

For the first few months, life at the New Way Toning Salon was very good for Kathy and her friend Martha Young. The two women enjoyed running the health club. Kathy—with her glasses,

neat, short hairstyle, sweatsuit, and sneakers—
looked the part of a hardworking woman with
her own business.

Soon this legitimate side of the business was
doing quite well. Kathy and Martha worked very
hard to build it up. The two women were worried
by the drug dealing in their back room, but without the narcotics gang backing the health club it
would never have happened.

Kathy continued turning a blind eye when
heavyset characters showed up with vans for de-
livery and collection at all times of the day and
night. For the first time in her adult life she had
enough money to pay the mortgage, feed and
clothe her children, and enjoy some of the better
things in life.

When business at the health club slipped a little, Mary O'Guinn and her brother Roy Vernon
Dean asked Kathy if she would begin delivering
marijuana herself. She agreed because they were
offering her more money to do it. And, with her
drunken husband Keith hitting rock bottom back
at home in St. Jacob, it seemed to make a lot of
sense.

Kathy Gaultney soon found herself driving
around with hundreds of thousands of dollars'
worth of pot plus wads of cash in the trunk of
her car. Who would bother stopping and searching a housewife from St. Jacob? She hardly
looked the part of a hardened drug dealer involved in one of the biggest drug supply net-
works in American criminal history.

As Kathy parked her car outside her cozy little
cottage in St. Jacob, she did not even bother to

take her valuable booty inside the house. It was better kept out of the way of her kids and husband Keith, who even warned her daughter Rachel to be careful about drugs.

"There's a lot of evil people out there who'll try to force you to take drugs. Just tell 'em no way," he told her one day, not realizing what Kathy was up to.

But Keith Gaultney could not come to terms with his own addiction—to alcohol. In his mind the damage he was inflicting on his own liver was not as morally wrong as smoking hash. Sometimes Kathy Gaultney felt like telling him that hash was probably less harmful than booze but she never plucked up the courage.

Then one morning, Keith Gaultney—sober for once—went outside to get a jack from his wife's car and discovered drugs and cash stashed in the boot. He returned to the house in a rage.

"Kathy. What the hell have you got in the trunk?"

Kathy Gaultney did not reply at first. She needed a moment to think about this. Should she admit to Keith they were drugs or should she try and deny they even belonged to her?

She concluded there was really no point in hiding the obvious. Kathy sat down on the bed beside her husband and started to tell him the truth. It just made Keith Gaultney even madder.

Now he had something on his wife, for a change. All those years of heavy drinking had put him in a vulnerable position as far as their relationship was concerned. Now he had the upper hand.

"Drugs? What the hell you doin' sellin' drugs?"

Kathy thought she had the perfect excuse.

"How else were we goin' to pay the mortgage, the bills, the kids' clothes?"

Keith Gaultney hated not being the main breadwinner in that family. Kathy was making him face facts—and it hurt.

"But we could have survived some other way."

Kathy Gaultney did not agree. It was time for some plain speaking in that household. Maybe the discovery of the drugs was a blessing in disguise? Perhaps now she could come out in the open and say what she had been thinking for years.

"There was no other way. You've lived off my money for months. I haven't noticed you complaining."

Keith Gaultney did not reply. He understood her point, but he would never accept that selling drugs was the answer. He'd never felt the urge to even try hash as a kid. Now his wife, the mother of his only son, was admitting that she was heavily involved in a vast drug ring.

For the following months Keith could barely bring himself to speak to his wife, and he sank deeper and deeper into an alcoholic abyss during which he'd let fly a tirade of abuse centered around the inevitable subject of drugs.

"How can you sit there and tell me that drugs don't harm people? How can you?"

Kathy Gaultney was getting mightily fed up. It was time for some home truths.

"Well, hash is hardly any more harmful than all that booze you drink."

Kathy was hitting back. She believed her narcotics overlords were only dealing in pot. Where was the harm in that?

But Keith Gaultney's attitude was unshakable. Nothing would convince him that hash might not be so bad. Kathy started to feel that he might even one day tell the authorities about her. He was *that* angry.

But it was Keith's drinking more than Kathy's drug dealing that was tearing the Gaultney family apart. It was a morning, noon and night-time addiction. Even when work offers came along for Keith he was too drunk to respond.

Kathy's life was exhausting. She would get home after a hard day running the beauty salon, followed by hours of precision-weighing hundreds of thousands of dollars' worth of cannabis. Yet she was still expected to make them all dinner. Bathe her son. Get both kids to bed *and* then attend to her husband's every whim and command. She was running out of patience.

Some nights she'd stay on at the shop in Collinsville and have a drink with her great friend and partner, Martha, because it was definitely preferable to going home to face Keith and the kids.

But Kathy knew things could not just go on like that forever. When she got home late one night in February, 1988, and Keith rounded on her and started threatening her, she snapped.

As Keith ranted and raved about "those damn

drug peddlers,'' she packed a suitcase, grabbed both the kids and headed out the front door. A few days later, she filed for divorce. But what disturbed her the most was that each time she tried to have a reasonable conversation with Keith on the phone, he would start up again about those drugs.

''I reckon the authorities would like to hear all about those sleazeballs you work for.''

Kathy did not like the sound of what she was hearing. The ramblings of a drunken, vindictive husband were one thing. But a threat to destroy everything she had built up so carefully was another matter altogether.

She knew from the tone of his voice that he was contemplating taking this whole business a much more dangerous stage further. At that moment she made up her mind to do something about it.

''It's the perfect weapon for a lady.''

The assistant in the gun shop in Collinsville might as well have been trying to sell Kathy Gaultney a piece of jewelry.

Kathy was examining a .22 Saturday night special.

As she handled the snub-nosed pistol over the store counter, she knew it was the right thing to do. The stress and strain of running a beauty salon, an illicit drugs factory and divorcing her alcoholic husband was driving her to desperate measures.

''Do ya think it'll stop my husband abusin' me?''

The clerk looked a little puzzled. But Kathy wanted reassurance.

"I can assure you, ma'am, that no husband in his right mind will mess with one of those things."

Next Kathy Gaultney enrolled at a nearby shooting range for expert training on how to handle that gun. Back home her husband continued to threaten to blow the whistle on her illegal activities.

Kathy didn't know if Keith would carry through with it, but she had a gut feeling he would. No one was going to destroy her life. She would see him go to hell rather than allow him to get away with ruining everything for her and the kids.

Back at their little house in St. Jacob, Keith Gaultney had become a very lonely, isolated character. Kathy and the kids had moved out to live in Collinsville. He had no company, except for bottles of booze. Perhaps it was not really that surprising when his addled, paranoid mind convinced him that the way to get back at Kathy was to blow the whistle on those evil drug barons who had destroyed their life together.

Keith Gaultney picked up the phone and dialed the directory inquiry service.

"Internal Revenue Service, please."

He only meant to scare Kathy into seeing sense and coming back with the kids. The IRS would rap her on the knuckles and then go after the really big boys. Keith Gaultney did not even consider the fact that the U.S. Drug Enforcement Agency would automatically get involved.

March 18, 1988, seemed like a pretty ordinary day at the New Way Toning Salon in Collinsville. There were a handful of women customers going through their $20-a-head skin toning session and no sign of the illegal activities that were a daily routine in the back room of the premises.

No one even noticed the black van parked up across the street from the beauty salon until six DEA agents smashed their way through the front and back exits of the salon. Kathy's first reaction was to deny any knowledge of the drug den hidden behind the main store. Under her breath she muttered, "You bastard, Keith. You bastard."

As the well-dressed officers made a clean sweep of the premises, Kathy and Martha looked on with blank expressions. Kathy was furious. She looked over at her friend and said, "Keith did this. I could kill him."

By the time the agents had taken away various pieces of evidence of the drug packaging that was taking place behind the salon, Kathy had already decided to get even.

"I know you did it, Keith. I just know."

Keith Gaultney didn't even bother to deny it when confronted by his wife shortly after that raid. Amazingly she had not been charged by the DEA because of the lack of evidence of actual drugs on the premises of the beauty salon.

Kathy's drug-smuggler bosses even decided that Kathy and Martha would have to continue dealing from their cars and homes rather than using the back room of the salon. The two women agreed because they needed the money.

However, Keith Gaultney still represented a threat to the operation, especially since the whole of St. Jacob now knew from local newspaper reports of the raid that his wife was a suspected drug peddler.

All it needed was another call from him to the IRS and then Kathy would undoubtedly end up in jail. But Keith Gaultney held back. He actually hoped that Kathy would stop her involvement in drugs following that DEA raid. He wanted them to get reconciled. But Kathy Gaultney was in way too deep.

A few weeks later, Keith Gaultney was delighted and certainly a tad surprised when Kathy announced she was moving back into their pretty little cottage in St. Jacob and putting the divorce plans on ice.

For the first few months after she reappeared, he even tried to slow down his drinking so they could resume a normal family life together with the kids. He was convinced the marriage was on the mend.

Kathy wasn't sure if Keith was worth going back to but she wanted to keep an eye on him.

Not surprisingly the booze battled its way back into Keith's life once more. Keith also realized that his wife was much more heavily involved with the Roy Vernon Dean drug cartel than he thought.

One day Keith Gaultney even told his wife,

''Drugs are goin' to be the death of us, Kathy. You mark my words.''

Keith Gaultney had a habit of putting his foot in his mouth. But this time he was putting ideas into his wife's head. She looked over at him, droning on and on through the alcohol and thought about that Saturday night special she'd purchased.

His drunken accusations were wearing her down. For almost a year she held back, but he kept mentioning the drugs, Then Kathy Gaultney finally cracked after yet another threat from Keith when she got back late from a drug supply run.

''One day, I'll go to them and then that'll stop that bastard Dean,'' slurred Keith at his wife.

On the early evening of September 22, 1989, Kathy told her daughter Rachel and a friend to go outside and play. Rachel and her friend had no money between them and wanted to go down to the late-night store and buy some sodas and a packet of chips.

So the two girls sat down in an empty salvage yard opposite the Gaultney house on Second Street and waited for Kathy Gaultney and Rachel's stepbrother Walter to leave on a shopping trip. The plan was to then slip in and steal a few dollars from Keith Gaultney's wallet. He was always so boozed up by about seven that he'd have collapsed in bed, out to the world.

As the two girls waited patiently for Kathy to leave the house, they could not have even suspected what was happening inside that property.

* * *

Kathy Gaultney looked down at the snoring, booze-sodden figure of the man who called himself her husband and just sneered. As he lay there in a drunken stupor, she felt no remorse for what she was about to do. She locked her son out of the bedroom and told him to wait in the hall before they went shopping. She had some unfinished business to attend to.

The .22 Saturday night special was rocksteady in her hand. She would not—and could not—turn back.

She cocked the gun, leaned down silently and pressed the barrel right into the fatty folds of skin on his forehead. Still he did not stir. He was out to the world.

She prodded the barrel one last time just to see if he noticed. No response. If he had stirred then, Kathy Gaultney might not have seen it through. But she presumed he'd hardly feel a thing because he was already out cold anyway.

Her finger tightened on the trigger. She placed her left hand over the gun to help steady it. She didn't want it rebounding back on her. Those lessons at the gun club had given her a good basic knowledge of the mechanics of guns.

Kathy pressed hard and felt the gun tremble as it fired. The bullet ripped the skin of his forehead and woke him from his drunken haze.

Kathy was alarmed by his consciousness. He was looking at her now with quizzical desperation etched on his face. She moved back a few inches and aimed again at his head.

Then he moved. He tried to speak. She fired from close range. This time the bullet tore a gaping hole in the side of his head and took off on a helter-skelter ride inside his brain.

His body slumped on the waterbed. Kathy Gaultney stood back and watched as his last few heartbeats pumped into oblivion. He was lying in exactly the same position he used to strike every evening after a heavy bout of drinking.

Without even a flicker of emotion, Kathy Gaultney began pulling out drawers from the closet next to the bed and dropped them onto her husband's corpse. She wanted it to look like a robbery gone tragically wrong.

Ten minutes later she left the house with her young son, completely unaware that her daughter Rachel was watching from across the street.

Rachel and her friend silently crept in through the back door of the house just in case they woke Keith Gaultney. The youngsters headed for the bedroom like two cat burglars on the prowl.

Rachel looked inside the bedroom where her stepfather lay shot to death. She presumed he was just asleep. She began searching the room for his wallet and completely ignored the drawers emptied over his body.

Rachel crept silently around the bedroom looking for his wallet. Once she found what she was looking for, she left the room, unaware that her stepfather was dead.

"Is that the police? My husband's been shot. You better come quickly."

Kathy Gaultney sounded distraught to the telephone operator who took her emergency call later that evening. She told officers she had returned home from a late-night shopping trip to find her husband shot dead in their bed. It looked like a robbery that had gone wrong.

As the paramedics, medical examiners, and assorted police mingled inside and outside the Gaultney house, one figure stepped back into the shadows and found herself examining her own conscience—Kathy's 13-year-old daughter Rachel.

Only a few hours earlier she had seen her mother leave that house with her stepbrother and she had seen what later transpired to be the body of her stepfather. She didn't know what to do.

After the police investigators pulled out some hours later, Rachel retreated to her little bedroom, haunted by the role she had played in the whole tragic scenario.

For those first few weeks after the murder of her husband, Kathy Gaultney cut a pretty confident figure in St. Jacob—still reeling from the first deliberate killing in the town's 100-year history.

People may have been whispering behind her back, but Kathy did not care. She had got rid of her drunken, nagging husband and that was all that mattered.

Even when a friend advised her to contact a lawyer in case police tried to haul her in for questioning, she was super cool about the whole business.

But daughter Rachel was not so relaxed. Three weeks later she called the police and told them what happened that fateful night.

A few hours later Kathy Gaultney motored

Dwight inmate Kathy Gaultney meets author Wensley Clarkson. (Wensley Clarkson)

The house in St. Jacob, Illinois where Kathy Gaultney murdered her husband. (Wensley Clarkson)

The Cottage at Dwight Correctional Center.
(Wensley Clarkson)

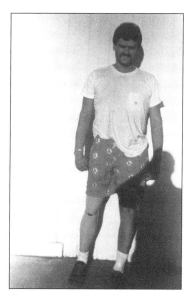

One-legged drug baron Roy Vernon Dean; Kathy Gaultney worked for his narcotics ring. (St. Jacob Police Department)

Mary O'Guinn persuaded Kathy Gaultney to go into "business" with her family. (St. Jacob Police Department)

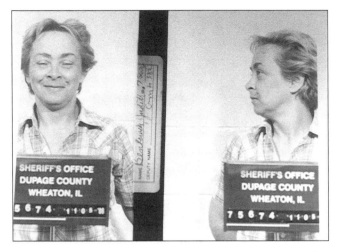

So happy: Judy Benkowski shortly after her arrest for the murder of her husband. (Addison Police Department)

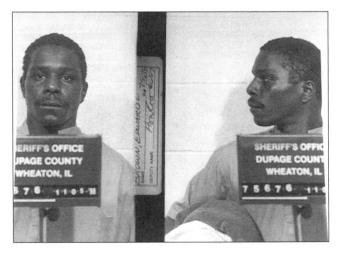

Pint-sized assassin Eddie Brown after he shot Clarence Benkowski to death. (Addison Police Department)

Happier times: Judy Benkowski marrying former neigh-
bor Clarence Jeske in 1991.
(Addison Police Department)

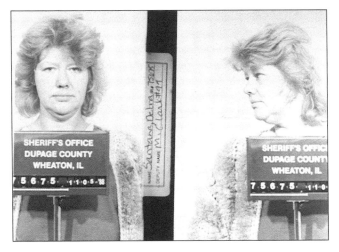

Judy's best friend and Brown's lover, Debra Santana.
(Addison Police Department)

Addison Detective Sergeant Tom Gorniak, whose investigative skills brought a speedy conclusion to the Benkowski murder case.
(Wensley Clarkson)

The grim entrance area to the Bedford Hills Correctional Facility, New York. (Wensley Clarkson)

Bedford Hills inmate Shenée Green with her daughter.
(Wensley Clarkson)

into nearby Edwardsville with a friend. Slowing down at a crossing, she even smiled when she spotted two of the state police detectives and an attorney leading the investigation into her husband's murder.

"Aren't you guys having a busy day?" she called out to them.

Kathy Gaultney was pushing her luck. But she did not realize that the case against her was now sufficient for a warrant to be issued for her arrest. Minutes later, police pulled up to the van she was traveling in and arrested her for the murder of her husband.

In April, 1990, Kathy Gaultney, then aged 34, was sentenced to life imprisonment after being found guilty of the first-degree murder of 35-year-old husband Keith.

Prosecuting attorney Don Weber told the court, "This crime was planned, but it wasn't planned well."

And, describing Kathy Gaultney's own daughter's role in her mother's conviction, he added, "In any crime, the inadvertent witness is the one thing you can't plan for."

Some months after her trial, Kathy Gaultney contacted authorities and agreed to provide inside information on the drug cartel she worked for with Martha Young.

Twelve people including Mary O'Guinn and her notorious one-legged drug baron brother Roy Vernon Dean were arrested and eventually given lengthy sentences for their involvement in one of the biggest narcotics rings in U.S. history.

Martha Young was also imprisoned as a result

of testimony from her best friend Kathy. However the two women still write to each other from the different facilities where they are incarcerated in Illinois. Kathy claims that they have remained friends despite everything.

But her trial left Kathy a broken woman in many ways.

"When the judge read the verdict I felt the blood drain from my face, but I forced myself to sit up straight, not to show any emotion," says Kathy now.

"I wasn't going to give them the satisfaction of seeing how much shock and pain they'd caused me."

What Kathy Gaultney maintains is dignity and determination. The press and prosecution interpreted her lack of response in court as coldness and remorselessness.

"They couldn't have been more wrong. But I was brought up not to make a show and dance of anything. So that's the way I am. I can't help it."

For Kathy and many of the other women inside Dwight, life is painfully monotonous.

"Being a woman in jail for more than half my life is the loneliest feeling in the world," says Kathy. "It doesn't shock people when it's a man because it's accepted that men are naturally more violent. I should know because my own husband behaved that way all the time.

"But to the public, women who've been sentenced for murder are monsters. We are put in places like this and largely ignored. We make folk feel uncomfortable because we could be anyone's wife, mother, grandmother. It's that simple.''

At one stage inside Dwight, Kathy took the familiar route of discovering religion inside prison but it didn't work.

''It's so easy to pick up a Bible and use religion to excuse our sins. God knows, there are so many women in this place doing exactly that. It is pathetic.

''In prison they become so-called Christians because they believe that then God will forgive them and that will somehow make it all better. Many of them make pacts with their family and friends to pray at a certain time each day. They stop whatever they're doing and say they pray for the strength to face whatever God has sent them.

''The truth is that religious studies simply enable inmates to get more freedom within the prison system. They would rather go to church than be locked down or working in the bathrooms. It doesn't seem the right reason to get into religion,'' says Kathy.

''How can you believe in God when he allows all this to happen? There's more evil in this place than you can imagine. And what's the point in having faith when you're already dead 'cause that's how I feel in here.''

For Kathy it is the waiting, the counting off of each day that is agonizing. It's not made any easier by the monotony and isolation that exists in Dwight, as in all prisons.

Kathy's day begins at 5:30 A.M. with biscuits and porridge. ''I wish they'd just let us sleep a little longer then the days would pass much quicker.''

She spends her mornings inside The Cottage reading, cleaning, and then preparing lunch alongside some of the other honor inmates who've been allowed to live in the detached building overlooked by the correctional facility fortress.

Even though the inmates are allowed to cook for themselves it doesn't make the meals any more appetizing. ''It's starch—it's cheap, makes you feel lethargic, and slows the brain, or so I believe,'' says Kathy.

''In the afternoon I try to take some exercise 'round the garden and get on with my duties keeping the living areas clean.''

Another meal follows in the late afternoon. Then Kathy reads, writes letters, or talks to the solitary guard who is based at the entrance to The Cottage. At 10 P.M. it's lights out. Some of the women inside The Cottage find solace with each other but many like Kathy often end up crying themselves to sleep.

''I cry when I'm depressed,'' she says. ''I miss my kids more than anything. Being away from them is the biggest punishment of all.

''The most depressing days are Christmas and their birthdays but I don't dare show my feelings or they'd put me on suicide watch. That's the worst thing that can happen. They take everything from you, even your soap.

''People wonder why there are so many suicides in prison. It's because for many there is no hope in sight and death can seem like a release from all the inner turmoil and anguish.

"It's like having an axe hanging over your head day and night. It never goes away . . . but you keep waiting for it to fall."

Meanwhile Gaultney herself insists that she did not carry out the murder of her drug informant husband. She maintains that he was killed by other members of the Roy Vernon Dean gang who wanted to silence Keith Gaultney before he helped authorities close down their drug cartel.

When I interviewed her in The Cottage at Dwight, she was still protesting her innocence and insisting that she would eventually succeed in overturning the jury's verdict.

In a hushed voice, as various other inmates walked freely around the inside of the building, she tells me, "I put up with a lot of shit from Keith but there's no way that I killed him."

As another woman inmate—also sentenced to life for murder—poured us each a cup of tea, Kathy went on: "I've done a lot of bad things in my life, but I ended up paying the price for working for an evil ring of drug smugglers. They killed Keith and then managed to get the police to arrest me. One day I'll prove the truth."

The protests of innocence usually fall on deaf ears in a place like Dwight.

SEVEN
Judy

JUDY BENKOWSKI IS ONE OF THE MOST UN-
likely killers you'll ever meet. She's very slightly
built, her eyes look in a permanent state of fear
like a deer caught in a car's headlights.

She flutters around The Cottage helping out
with the dishes, smiling at everyone but obviously a very quiet, reserved lady. It's difficult to
imagine the crime that she committed.

The shrill of a bell tingling loudly in the distance
meant only one thing to Judy Benkowski—her
husband was demanding something yet again.

Clarence Benkowski was overweight and
overbearing. All his life he had been number one
in their often miserable household. Even after re-
tiring from his job as a welder, he expected to
be waited upon hand and foot.

So when his sick and aged mother decided to
move in, the workload on Judy became almost
too much to handle. They both treated her like

dirt. She never got a moment to herself. It was a miserable existence, but Judy didn't often complain. That just wasn't her way of doing things.

Often those two obese specimens would sit in the armchairs in the living room of their neat, detached suburban home at 508 South Yale Avenue, Addison, on the outskirts of Chicago, for hours without moving. That was when the little bell they used rang the most. An endless stream of demands always followed.

RING—"Get me a coffee," said one.

RING—"Get me a beer," said the other.

RING—"This coffee's cold, get me another."

RING—"This beer's not cold enough. They should be kept in the icebox."

And so it went on, and on, and on. Judy had no time for a proper job and she had only a small handful of friends in the entire world. Her occupation was looking after those two leeches and her two sons.

Not surprisingly, Judy got pretty desperate at times. Her life was relentless and so unenjoyable. She'd often cry herself to sleep at night, wondering when it would ever end. Occasionally, Clarence would drunkenly attempt sex with her. It certainly wasn't making love. He was very forceful and it seemed more like rape than anything else.

Clarence made her fondle him and then—the moment he was ready—she would just lie there and listen to him grunting. Often she'd try to think of other things, like the next day's shopping. At least it was usually over in minutes, if not seconds. But there was so much pain involved. Not love. It was the sort of pain that inevitably occurs when an overweight old man forces himself on a slightly built, five-foot-tall woman more than 20 years his junior. They might have been husband and wife in law, but they were total strangers in every other sense of the word.

One day Clarence decided to spice up *his* sex life by purchasing a waterbed. Typically, it was the cheapest one he could find and had the unpleasant side effect of being so overfilled with water that it made them both feel extremely seasick.

Judy would lie there during sex with an awful, overwhelming sensation of waves rocking them up and down as if they were on a boat bobbing across the ocean.

But there was one advantage; she felt so nauseous within seconds of Clarence starting, that he would often stop rather than risk being barfed on.

Clarence's attitude toward sex was much the same as his outlook on life: Men ruled the household. Women were there to honor and obey. He didn't care about Judy's feelings. He just wanted four big, square meals a day and an occasional fuck on demand.

For almost 20 years Judy put up with the misery. What else could she do? She had no career. No existence outside those four walls. She had been trapped for so long she had forgotten what it was like to enjoy herself. Then she became friendly with a pretty blonde neighbor and the two women began enjoying occasional lunches together.

"You cannot let him treat you like this. You've got to do something about it, Judy.'

Debra Santana was outraged by her friend Judy's total acceptance of her distressing marital situation. She'd heard a number of horror stories from Judy. How could a husband treat his wife so badly? Debra knew *she'd* never put up with it for a second.

"But," Judy explained, in her quiet, reserved way, "what can I do? I have nowhere to go. No money. I've got no choice."

Debra disagreed and told Judy she would help her. Debra was a striking blonde, aged 32, with a fun-loving attitude toward life. She had suffered during her own marriage and took the easy way out—divorce. Now she was enjoying everything that Judy had long since given up hope of ever having. She wanted Judy to have a piece of the action before it was too late.

Debra even had an athletic, African-American lover who gave her all-around satisfaction and never treated her badly. Debra loved to regale Judy with stories about his prowess between the sheets. She was even rather proud that he had a *criminal* record.

Judy was very envious of Debra's lifestyle. She longed to feel warmth, passion, and true love again from a man. Judy knew Debra was right when she said she had to do something. But what?

Clarence Benkowski, a strict Catholic, would

not even discuss the subject of divorce with his wife. And there was no question of them leading separate lives either.

Clarence believed he owned Judy lock, stock, and barrel. She was his woman. If he wanted instant sex he should get it. If he wanted to insult her he could. If he wanted her to be his slave no one could stop him. He made a point of telling Judy all this on numerous occasions.

Judy's friend Debra may have been 13 years younger than Judy but she was becoming increasingly influential in her life. The more they talked about Debra's adventures, the more Judy began to realize how desperate she was to end her own misery.

"But what can I do about him?" Judy asked her friend one day.

"I've got an idea," replied Debra. "I'm gonna introduce you to my boyfriend Eddie."

Eddie Brown had given Debra all the sexual satisfaction she had ever craved. Even fully clothed, his muscular torso virtually popped his shirt buttons. Judy Benkowski certainly appreciated why Debra so enjoyed her handsome stud, but she was surprised Eddie was so short—just five-foot-three-inches tall. In fact, Debra towered over him by a good four inches.

"Not only is Eddie great in bed, but he's also goin' to help you with your problem, Judy," chipped in Debra when all three met up for lunch at a restaurant near Judy's home. No reference was made to Eddie's status as a virtual dwarf.

Over the following couple of hours Debra tried

to convince Judy that Eddie was the perfect man for a very special job. It was a mission that required a certain degree of careful planning—the assassination of Clarence Benkowski.

Eddie Brown had earlier assured his lover Debra he could murder Judy's husband with ''no trouble.'' He'd told her the job would cost $5,000.

But Judy Benkowski had her doubts. She was a regular law-abiding homemaker and this murderous scheme did not sit easy with her. Her conscience was troubling her. How could she even contemplate murdering another human being? It seemed all wrong. She hesitated.

''Maybe we should re-think all this?''

There was brief silence from her two accomplices.

''What?'' said Debra. ''You can't change your mind. It's gotta be done. Come on. Let's do it!''

Debra made a feeble high-five, but only Eddie responded.

He then chipped in, ''Yeah. It'll be easy. We can make it look like a break-in. No problem.''

Judy wasn't a strong-willed woman at the best of times. She was feeling as if she'd got in too deep already.

But this was her only possible escape route from a miserable life. It was the answer to all her problems. It might seem drastic, but that fat pig of a husband deserved it. He had treated her like dirt for too long. Now it was her turn. Revenge would seem sweet. For the first time in her life Judy decided to be strong.

''Okay. How we goin' to do it?'' asked Judy, surprised at her own positiveness.

It was mid-October, 1988, and Halloween was fast approaching. Judy said she had a great idea. Turning to Eddie, she said, "I'll get you [Eddie] a real scary costume. You're so short you'll look just like a kid out trick-or-treatin'. Then you'll knock on the door, Clarence will answer, and you'll shoot him. Bang. Bang. Trick or treat!"

Debra and Eddie looked bemused. It was a ridiculous plan. Perhaps Judy had been trapped in that house for longer than they thought. She'd lost the plot.

"That's the weirdest plan I ever heard," said Eddie, scratching his chin and trying to be polite.

"No, it ain't. It'll work like a dream. I know it," insisted Judy, who didn't doubt her own wisdom for a second.

And she was adamant. She clearly relished the ghoulish, theatrical elements of the plan, and even laughed excitedly as she continued to describe the plot.

"He never wants to give anything to the kids who come knocking at the door. Well, this time he's goin' to get a real surprise."

The earlier, hesitant Judy had now turned into a hard-nosed would-be killer intent on getting into the mood to murder. Her transformation even surprised her two friends. The risks involved were being outweighed by the fast-approaching scenario—a new life without Clarence. Judy was feeling happier than she had for years.

"But hang on there, Judy," said Eddie. "Trick-or-treaters don't gun down homeowners. The cops would know it was a contract hit straight off, and they'd get on to us for sure."

Eddie wanted to defuse this particular plan because it was riddled with holes. He may have agreed to murder this woman's husband and the guy sounded like he deserved it, but Judy's scheme was crazy.

Judy ignored Eddie's protestations. "The cops will think some crazy trick-or-treater is out there blasting innocent people to death. They'll never think it was a hit."

Debra and Eddie glanced at each other and shrugged their shoulders.

They should have fought her on the finer points of this murderous mission but she was pulling the purse strings.

"You're the boss, lady," said Eddie. Jobless and just out of jail, he needed the money, so he wasn't about to blow the contract, whatever the risks.

So it was, on Halloween night of 1988, Eddie Brown—dressed in a luminous skeleton leotard—allowed Judy and Debra to adjust a ghoulish latex face mask they had bought for him at the local store. They were all huddled in the front room of Debra's house just up the street from the Benkowskis'. Eddie still had serious doubts about dressing up as a kid and going out trick-or-treating before blasting a fat, lazy husband to death.

To make matters worse, the latex mask was very uncomfortable. His skin was sweating and the mask was squeaking every time he changed facial expressions. The two women had insisted on getting one that covered his entire face so that no one could see what color his skin was. But it was so airless behind that mask that Eddie kept having to remove it in order to breathe. He was gasping for air even before he left the house.

There were other operational problems as well.

"This is crazy," moaned Eddie. "I can't even see properly out of the eye slits."

His voice was so badly muffled by the mask, the two women did not even hear him at first.

So he yelled, "I SAID THIS IS CRAZY."

If Eddie was going to have to shout this loudly to be heard, then he'd probably alert the entire street when he went knocking on Clarence Benkowski's front door to announce his trick-or-treating routine.

The two women ignored Eddie's pleas to abort the mission and he was pushed out into the tree-lined residential street.

Within seconds Eddie's face dropped. Well, it would have if he had not had that latex mask on. There were children wandering up and down the street in trick-or-treating disguises. It seemed like the entire child population of Addison had decided to hit South Yale at exactly the same time.

Eddie ripped off the mask in a fit of fury and stood there in his white skeleton costume jumping up and down on the spot. The two women looked out at him with infuriated expressions on their faces.

"I am not doing this. I can't start shooting at a guy in front of all these kids. I'll never get away with it."

Judy was incensed. She was just a few hours away from never having to see that ugly hulk of a husband again and Eddie had ruined everything. She rushed outside.

"We have to do it, Eddie. You cut a deal."

"Don't get me wrong, Judy. I will kill him. But not tonight. It'd be crazy and we'd all end up in jail."

Judy reluctantly agreed.

"Okay. But we gotta do it soon."

"Don't worry. We'll do it. I promise."

RING—"Where's my breakfast?"

RING—"Come on, I'm hungry."

RING . . . RING . . . RING . . .

Clarence Benkowski was performing his usual pre-breakfast routine the same way he had for the previous 20 years. At least his mother was away at a relative's so Judy didn't have to tolerate her. In the kitchen, Judy muttered quietly under her breath, "*Coming, sweetheart.*"

If Clarence had not been so incredibly lazy, he might have got up from the breakfast table where he was slouched and lumbered into the kitchen to witness Judy pouring the contents of twenty packets of sleeping pills into his coffee.

Instead he just kept on ringing.

RING—"Move your ass, woman. I'm *hungry.*"

Ringing that bell yet again marked the beginning of the end of his life. For it guaranteed Judy felt no guilt as she emptied the contents of the packets and then swilled them around in his coffee. The more he rang the bell, the better she felt about killing him. Just to contemplate the end of such an awful era in her life was a wonderful feeling.

Judy's only error was to throw the empty pill packets into the trash can before moving towards the dining area with a new spring in her step, a new bounce in her walk.

"There you go, sweetheart."

She hadn't called him that for years.

Judy sat down at the breakfast table and sipped quietly at her tea, but her eyes kept drifting upwards and across the table towards Clarence. He hadn't even touched that coffee yet.

But Clarence was a creature of habit. He liked to gulp down his fried eggs first and stuff some toast in that big fat mouth of his. Judy knew that cup of coffee would soon be lifted to his lips. *Be patient. Relax. He's going to drink it. All in good time. All in good time.*

The Chicago Sun-Times was spread across the table in front of Clarence, as it always was each morning. Something caught his eye. He stopped eating and gasped at the sports results.

He'd never made conversation with Judy over breakfast, or at any other time for that matter. Clarence wasn't about to break the habit of a lifetime. That cup of coffee remained untouched. Judy's initial burst of excitement was changing to desperation. *Come on! Come on! Get on with it!*

"Sweetheart." For some weird reason she used *that* word again. "Sweetheart, drink your coffee or it'll get cold."

For a split second, Clarence looked at his wife quizzically. She *never* spoke at breakfast. Why the hell was she making him drink his coffee?

Judy sensed his hesitation and was annoyed with herself for being so obvious.

She did not dare look up again in case he caught her eye.

But, as with most things in Clarence's life, he gave his wife's odd behavior only brief consideration before allowing his stomach to rule his brain.

The harsh slurping noise was music to Judy's ears. She opened her eyes once more to see him gulping it down at a furious rate, trying to wash all that food down his huge, ugly gullet.

Another cup of coffee followed in quick succession. Judy felt the relief running through her veins. She sighed quietly to herself. It was one of the most satisfying moments of her life.

Not long after this, Clarence started to feel very drowsy.

"I don't feel so good. I think I'll lie down a while."

Eddie had provided precise instructions on how many sleeping tablets she should feed him. Just enough to knock him into a deep slumber rather than complete unconsciousness. That way no one would be able to tell later he had been drugged.

Clarence lumbered to his feet and struggled toward the bedroom. He collapsed just as he got to that wretched over-filled waterbed. Judy crept into the room after him—just to make sure. The only movement were the waves of water rippling under the sheet. Then Judy phoned Debra and told her, "He's asleep."

Judy slammed down the phone and awaited her two accomplices.

Debra was the first to arrive at the house. She hugged Judy warmly. The two women sat down side-by-side on the couch in the front room and waited for Eddie. They heard the back door opening.

In complete silence, Judy handed Eddie her husband's World War Two Luger pistol and motioned him toward the master bedroom. They did not want to risk waking Clarence.

Debra meanwhile put on a pair of stereo headphones and began listening to heavy rock music. She wanted to blot out the noise of the gunfire when it happened.

The two women stayed on the couch. Eddie had told them earlier that he would use a pillow to muffle the sound of the gun, but Judy still heard the dull thuds of three bullets being pumped into her husband on the waterbed.

But there was more work to be done. They had to make it look like a burglary that had gone wrong. The two women and Eddie Brown began tearing the house apart. They pulled drawers of clothes out and spread them all over the bed where Clarence lay. Miraculously, the waterbed remained intact despite the rain of bullets. Judy was relieved because it would have caused such a mess if it had leaked everywhere.

Meanwhile Eddie continued smashing the place up to make it look like a genuine burglary. But this proved more stressful to Judy than the murder of her husband.

"No. Not the china, please."

Judy angrily forbade Eddie from destroying her vast collection of china memorabilia which she had lovingly assembled over many years. It was one of the few possessions in that house she cared about.

"But this is supposed to look like a robbery," said Eddie.

"You don't have to wreck my china," replied Judy dryly.

Eddie shrugged his shoulders. She was the boss.

Just before Eddie left, Judy handed him one thousand dollars in cash as his first installment. She also allowed Eddie to take two rings from a jewelry drawer. The rest of the cash would be given to him within a week.

Seconds later Eddie was gone.

The two women embraced. They had done it. They had gotten rid of the husband from hell. Now there was a big wide world out there waiting to be conquered. Judy Benkowski's new life was about to begin.

The Italian restaurant where Judy and Debra went to celebrate that same evening was so crowded that they went virtually unnoticed at first. The only unusual thing was that they ordered a bottle of very expensive white wine, which meant their toast to one another did raise a few eyebrows.

"To us. Long may we live without husbands."

The two women chuckled like naughty schoolgirls.

And it wasn't just a new life of freedom that

Judy was looking forward to. She believed Clarence's life insurance would be worth at least $100,000 and then there was the $150,000 house with no mortgage.

Judy Benkowski intended to be a very merry widow indeed. But first they needed to get back to the house and report the murder.

"He's been murdered. He's been murdered."

Judy's screeching tones on the phone sounded very convincing to Addison cop, Detective Sergeant Tom Gorniak. He had been patched through to the Benkowski home after the nearby police station had received an emergency call from Debra and Judy, who told an operator they'd discovered Clarence shot dead on their return from a shopping trip.

In a bizarre three-way conference call between his patrol car, the police station switchboard, and Judy, Gorniak tried to establish what had happened, as he drove at high speed to South Yale Avenue.

By the time Gorniak rolled up at the house, paramedics had already arrived. The detective consoled the two women and got a uniformed officer to escort them from the property.

Then he began a detailed inspection of the premises. Gorniak knew he could not disturb anything until the crime scene technicians arrived, but he was well aware that this was the best time to look around because everything was untouched and exactly as it had been at the time of the murder.

He soon became rather puzzled by certain aspects of the crime.

The victim's body lay slumped in bed as if he had been taking an afternoon nap. How could he have slept through the noise of an intruder who then leaned over him and fired three bullets into his head at close range?

Gorniak also knew that few burglars would do that. Most just get the hell out of a house the moment they are disturbed. Their first response is usually to run—not shoot.

No, thought Gorniak, this victim was asleep when he was shot. He did not even have time to turn around and see who his killer was.

Then the policeman noticed the clothes thrown from the drawers over the body. That meant the killer had ransacked the room *after* the shooting. It did not make sense. The intruder would have got out of there as fast as possible following the murder.

Gorniak had been a policeman for 10 years. He knew how dangerous it was to draw any conclusions at such an early stage in a murder investigation, but this looked like a contract killing.

He decided to carry out some gentle questioning of the bereaved wife at Addison police station that evening.

"Did your husband have any enemies, Mrs. Benkowski?"

"No," Judy replied. "He had no enemies."

Gorniak was not convinced. He wanted Judy to stay on at the police station for a little longer that evening.

Judy agreed because she did not want to appear to be hindering the police inquiries in any way.

That night Gorniak and his colleague Detective Mike Tierney continued to question the widow. Something was wrong with the original prognosis.

Judy, meanwhile, was getting edgy. She had to tell them something. Maybe a half truth would solve her problems.

"I did see someone outside the house this morning," she recalled anxiously to the two detectives.

Gorniak and Tierney raised their eyebrows. They wondered why she hadn't mentioned this before.

Judy then described in detail how as she returned from her shopping trip with her friend Debra, they had seen this extremely short, stocky black man.

"He seemed to be running away from the house," explained Judy.

The two officers were very surprised. They began to pull in the reins a little bit and decided to haul Judy's friend Debra Santana in for questioning. As the detectives waited with Judy for her friend to arrive, they tried an old and trusted technique.

"It would help us if you could tell us everything you know," said Gorniak. "Even the details that don't seem relevant."

Judy hesitated. She had a lot on her mind.

"I think I knew the black guy who was running from my house. His name is Eddie Brown. He's Debra's boyfriend."

Tom Gorniak and Mike Tierney looked at each other. Within a few hours Judy, Debra, and Eddie had all made full and frank confessions.

In September, 1989, Judy Benkowski cried when she was sentenced to 100 years in prison for hiring hitman Eddie Brown to murder her husband.

Du Page County prosecutor Michael Fleming had argued that Judy should receive the death penalty. But Judge Brian Telander ruled that there were mitigating factors that "precluded the imposition of the death penalty."

These included no prior criminal record, numerous health problems, and several character witnesses who testified on her behalf.

Fleming described the sentence—which meant Judy would not be eligible for parole until she was 97—as "fair and appropriate. She claimed she wanted a divorce and he wouldn't go along, but she never even talked to a lawyer about it."

On August 31, 1991, Judy married sweetheart Clarence Jeske at the Dwight Correctional Institute. The couple had first met before her husband was murdered but they both insisted their relationship did not begin until after the killing.

By a strange twist of fate, Jeske now lives in that same house where Clarence was murdered, on South Yale Avenue. He has even been made legal guardian of Judy's two children by his marriage to Judy.

In 1996 Judy Benkowski died after a long illness. They still remember her with great fondness at Dwight.

"She couldn't harm a fly. She was a real lady

and she should never have been in jail,'' says
one inmate.

Many other staff and prisoners feel precisely
the same way about Judy Benkowski. May she
rest in peace . . .

EIGHT
Patty

PATTY COLUMBO'S DARK HAIR AND GOOD FIG-
ure catch the eye the moment any male walks
into The Cottage, at the Dwight Correctional
Center. Prisoner number C77200 is well turned
out, slinks between the living rooms with an air
of confidence that is not shared by many of the
other inmates.

As she leans down to put a cup of hot steaming
coffee on the table in front of me it's impossible
not to smile back at her, even though there is
something dark and distant about those deep, almost black, saucerlike eyes.

As she walks away another inmate whispers in
my ear, "That's Patty. You wanna keep well
away from her. She's the most famous killer in
here. She ain't ever goin' to get outta here."

At that moment Patty Columbo turns and
smiles back in my direction. I nervously try to
avoid her gaze. The woman inmate sitting next
to me laughs.

"Don't even think about it. She's the most evil woman I ever did meet."

But the details of Patty Columbo's crime tend to lend credence to those words.

After Patty Columbo hooked up with Frank DeLuca her relationship with the rest of her family rapidly deteriorated. At that time Patty had been 16 and DeLuca 36. Patty fought with her father because she wanted to drop out of her junior year at Elk Grove Village High School to work full-time in a local drugstore owned by DeLuca. She called her parents filthy names when they tried to discipline her and soon moved in with her lover.

Mr. Columbo eventually asked his daughter and her boyfriend to visit the family house for a peace conference. But the couple never showed up and an infuriated Mr. Columbo tracked them down to the drugstore parking lot.

Angry words were exchanged and Mr. Columbo waved a rifle at the couple. It was unloaded but Patty and DeLuca did not know that. Patty screamed and ran for cover while her lover tried to grapple the gun from Mr. Columbo. Then Mr. Columbo smashed the rifle butt into DeLuca's face sending teeth and blood flying.

Patty reported the incident to the police at the time and her father was picked up and arrested and spent the night in jail on assault charges. Soon afterwards Mr. Columbo bought Patty a car as a peace offering but DeLuca and his daughter refused to drop the charges so he angrily repossessed the vehicle. Charges were eventually dropped because DeLuca did not follow through with the complaint.

Then Mr. Columbo cut his daughter's inheritance from $100,000 to $5,000 in his will. He left the bulk of his estate to his son, although if Michael died then the primary beneficiary would once again be Patty. The estate included an $80,000 life insurance policy.

Patty was infuriated by her parents and began casting around for a hitman to kill them. One friend introduced her to 24-year-old Lanyon R. Mitchell, a former clerk in the Cook County Sheriff's Department. He then introduced Patty to his pal, 34-year-old Roman Sobczynski, a civil service recruitment officer for the Cook County Personnel Department and also a former sheriff's deputy. They seemed perfect candidates for the job of murdering the Columbos.

But the two men were more interested in getting attractive Patty into bed than going through with the hit. Patty promised a $50,000 fee from her inheritance and said they could have sex with her whenever they wanted. There was only one condition—she insisted they could only have anal sex with her because she was keeping herself for longtime lover DeLuca.

Meanwhile Frank DeLuca was openly delighted by the prospect of a massive injection of money. He told friends he was planning to buy a boat, pay off his wife in a generous divorce settlement and buy a huge mansion to share with Patty.

Patty even provided the two supposed "hitmen" with detailed files on each of her family members including their appearance, personal habits, and travel and work schedules. Patty also listed their places of birth, hair color, style, height, weight, and color of eyes, as well as their hobbies. She mentioned that her mother had been married before and included details of her brother's motorcycle club and CB call sign.

Only vague details of the family cars were provided because Patty didn't know their precise year of manufacture or license plate numbers. "And watch out for Gigi the poodle. She bites," warned Patty.

Photos of each family member plus a carefully sketched floor plan of the house were also included.

Patty eventually made the first down payment on the contract and began taking part in sexual threesomes with the two men. The two fake hitmen enjoyed the sex but kept complaining that she hadn't yet provided them enough money up front.

Patty got very irritated by their games and once pulled a loaded Derringer from her purse and waved it at Mitchell.

"See how easy it is to kill someone?" she said menacingly. "All you have to do is pull the trigger."

Then she called Mitchell "chickenshit Lannie."

"You got till Christmas. Make it a special present for me," she told the two men following yet another anal-sex session.

But five months after these sexual liaisons began, the two men decided to walk away from the plan. They even refused to return Patty's telephone calls.

Over in Elk Grove, Patty's parents were growing increasingly concerned by their daughter's erratic behavior. She made threats against them. They changed the locks on the doors of their house and dropped their listing from the local phonebook.

Then a man tried to get into Mrs. Columbo's car at a set of traffic lights. She got away unharmed but Mr. Columbo immediately bought her a pistol to keep in the vehicle and purchased another weapon for himself that he kept in a nightstand drawer in the master bedroom.

A few weeks later officers from the Elk Grove police called at the family house to tell the Columbos they had located a stolen car registered to them.

The brown Thunderbird was discovered in a street in a South Side black ghetto. It had been stripped of tires, CB radio, and just about everything else that could be easily carried away.

When the Elk Grove officers got no reply at the house they looked through the windows of the neatly kept $65,000 brick bi-level, ranch-style house and saw that a break-in of some kind had been committed. They got in through an open side door and stumbled upon what looked more like an abattoir than a home in Middle America.

The corpse of Frank Columbo, 43, lay on the living room carpet surrounded by blood, tissue, and shattered teeth. His skull had been viciously smashed, he had multiple stab wounds, his throat was slit from ear to ear, and he had been shot four times through each cheek, his mouth, and—execution style—behind the left ear. Furniture was turned over and blood was splattered on a nearby wall. This was a murderous assault of great intensity and anger.

But not even a gun, knife, and bludgeon were enough for these deranged killers. A lighted cigarette had even been stubbed out on his chest. Mr. Columbo's clothes were found in the bedroom suggesting that he had been first disturbed in his bed by the intruders.

Then investigators stumbled upon the body of Mr. Columbo's attractive 41-year-old wife lying just along the hallway bathroom. Her skull was crushed, she'd been shot between the eyes, her throat was slit, and she'd been repeatedly stabbed.

Mrs. Columbo's nightgown and robe had been ripped open and her underwear was pulled down to her ankles. Only later did it emerge that no sexual assault had taken place. She seemed to have been surprised by her killers while sitting in the bathroom reading a newspaper and smoking a cigarette.

But worse was still to come. In an upstairs bedroom was the body of their son Michael, dressed in blood-drenched nightclothes. He'd been shot between the eyes and his head smashed by a heavy object. Michael's face, neck, and body had been stabbed nearly 100 times—some wounds were deep while others had barely pierced his skin.

Makeshift blood-stained weapons were also recovered including a pair of sewing scissors, a knife, and the heavy base of a bowling trophy. Many of the cuts on the arms of the victims were defensive wounds which implied that they all put up a fearsome struggle before being murdered. There must have been at least two intruders.

The killers had got into the house through an automatic garage door, then they'd forced a lock on a door leading into the family room.

Sole survivor of this orgy of violence was the family poodle, Gigi. The animal whimpered in a blood-soaked corner of the living room while investigators and crime technicians began the grim task of gathering evidence.

It then emerged that the only family member still alive was the couple's pert, dark-haired 19-year-old daughter Patty, a willowy teenager with a penchant for figure-hugging clothes.

To her new neighbors Patty was a flamboyant girl who wore masses of makeup and was frequently seen around the apartment complex wearing revealing thigh-high miniskirts and high boots. She even boasted to a couple of neighbors that she modeled sexy underwear for Frederick's of Hollywood.

Patty also had a penchant for extremely short, skintight leather hotpants and flimsy blouses which she often wore in winter with a long fur-trimmed coat that flapped open to reveal her shapely legs. She told one man she met she was from Georgia and intended to open a modeling business. But Patty always made time to baby-sit in the complex. She needed the money.

Patty had tall, willowy, extremely noticeable looks which greatly contrasted with her lover DeLuca. He was short, sweaty, and bony. But he was renowned as a real charmer with the ladies. He wore immaculate leisure suits and shoes with high heels to make him look taller. Neighbors actually presumed that Patty and DeLuca were married.

Patty handled the news of her family's slaughter with incredible calm. She told police the murders must have been committed by a bunch of kids high on drugs. She even mentioned that the slayings reminded her of the dreadful Charles Manson-inspired slaughter of five people, including Sharon Tate, in Hollywood just a few years earlier.

In Elk Grove Village, residents locked up their doors and windows because they feared a team of vicious killers was stalking the neighborhood. Some bought guns to protect themselves, and business at local shooting ranges tripled following the Columbo killings.

At first, police believed there might be a link between the murders at the Columbo house on East Brantwood and a string of drug-related killings that had swept the nation since the Manson crimes.

Chicagoans were still reeling from the horrendous crimes of Texas drifter Richard Benjamin Speck who stumbled upon a dormitory housing nine student nurses on the city's South Side. Speck strangled and stabbed eight of the girls to death, and raped one during a drug- and drink-induced frenzy. Only one of the nurses escaped the massacre by rolling under a bed and hiding.

But there was one aspect of the killings of the Columbos that seriously troubled investigators. Many of the valuables inside the house were untouched even though the house had been ransacked. Columbo's will and $4,000 in cash remained inside the safe which hadn't been broken into. Not even the television, radios, silver, expensive jewelry, or any other valuable items had been taken. Mr. Columbo's rifle was ignored by the killers as were the expensive diamond rings on his wife's fingers.

The only objects definitely taken were two CB radios, two handguns, the heavy base of a floor lamp and the two family cars. The second car was eventually discovered abandoned on Chicago's West Side some days after the bodies were found.

The cigarette burns to Mr. Columbo's chest were very significant as were the scores of shallow stab wounds on his son and the apparent rape of Mrs. Columbo. Maybe they were tortured but simply refused to reveal where everything was hidden? Or was this some kind of personal vendetta?

Dr. Robert J. Stein performed the autopsies on the victims' bodies and concluded, ''There certainly appeared to be a lot of hate on display here.''

To add to the confusion, rumors began flying around that Mr. Columbo was a Mob-connected loan shark or drug baron. A few months before his death he had kept $30,000 in the wall safe. Surnames of locally known hoods were also discovered written in a notebook in the house.

An anonymous caller then tipped off police that Mr. Columbo was a silent partner in a local Mob-backed company. Certainly, he did seem to live a very luxurious lifestyle considering his annual salary was only supposed to be $25,000.

Seven days after the slayings a typewritten letter arrived at the Elk Grove Village Police Department. The writer claimed he was one of the mobsters named in the Columbo notebook. He said he had overheard two well-known contract killers discussing how they were going to settle a score with Frank Columbo.

Friends, family, and neighbors insisted that Columbo was a law-abiding citizen and daughter Patty even called a Chicago newspaper to complain about the stories suggesting her father was linked to organized crime. She sobbed as she told a reporter her father was an honest, hardworking man who would never lie. She also said she feared for her own safety and had changed the locks on the doors of her apartment and got a German shepherd. She gave her profession to the newspaper as a model and cosmetician.

The police eventually established that Columbo was nothing more than a hardworking shipping manager for Western Auto, a chain of auto accessory stores in Chicago.

It then emerged that the only serious brush with the law by a member of the Columbo family involved Patty. After moving in with DeLuca she was arrested for credit card deception. Her father bailed her out and she was eventually placed on probation.

Autopsy results confirmed that the Columbos had died about midnight on Tuesday, May 4, a couple of hours after returning from dining at a restaurant in nearby Arlington Heights. The bodies had been in the house for three days before police broke in. Ballistics tests also showed that the bullet wounds were inflicted with a .32 caliber handgun.

Then Michael J. Dunkle, a nephew of Mrs. Columbo, came forward and told investigators he had phoned the house on May 5 and spoken to a woman whom he believed to have been his aunt.

This baffled police because they knew the Columbos were dead by then. Did the killers stay in the house for at least six hours? Or had they returned to the scene of the killings later?

Detectives began probing Mr. Columbo's enemies closer to home. It was then they discovered he had been feuding with Patty since the day she started dating DeLuca three years earlier.

At the funeral of her murdered parents and brother, Patty Columbo upset her Catholic relatives by insisting their bodies should be immediately cremated.

Whispers that Patty and DeLuca might have been behind the killings also began to surface. Then one of Patty's girlfriends told her own father that Patty had tried to hire two hitmen to rub out her parents. Elk Grove Village police put Patty's nervous girlfriend under a 24-hour armed guard.

Investigators soon located supposed "hitmen" Mitchell and Sobczynski. The following day

Patty was arrested and accused of the murders of her parents and brother. DeLuca was taken into protective custody but not immediately charged.

In a search of Patty's apartment her Derringer gun was discovered although it was not the same caliber as the weapon used to shoot her family members. However, among other possessions were pornographic movies starring DeLuca with another attractive woman a few years older than Patty. There were also explicit photographs of the leggy teenager.

Within hours of her arrest Patty Columbo gave investigators and a state attorney a nine-page statement admitting that she had plotted her family's execution the previous October and had even taken Mitchell on a dry run, but she insisted she only wanted the "hitmen" to rough up her father because of the beating he had earlier given DeLuca.

"To begin with, my father was the only one I wanted hit, but they said if he went, my mother would have to go too," she told police. "I said okay as long as my brother was not hurt."

She claimed the hitmen said they were going to plant a bomb in the Columbos' car, but she called that off when her father's attitude towards DeLuca softened.

"Frank didn't know," she said. "I never told him about the contract."

Then Elk Grove Police Department investigator Raymond Rose confronted Patty with the dossier she had suppled the two hitmen. She admitted she wrote it but said, "I don't think they did it."

When Rose showed Patty sexually explicit photos of herself in various poses with her German shepherd dog, Duke, she said she had different feelings about morality from her police interrogators. She even admitted that she and DeLuca had sent their names and descriptions to numerous swingers magazines because they wanted to swap sexual partners.

Then Patty claimed her father had put a contract out on the life of DeLuca. She quoted her father as saying there would be "no marriage because there would be no Frank DeLuca."

Patty Columbo was formally charged with three counts of murder and one count of conspiracy to murder. DeLuca—locked in another part of the same jail—and his teenage mistress expressed their love for one another through messages delivered by other inmates.

Police continued collecting further evidence linking the two lovers to the slayings of the Columbo family. The two so-called "hitmen" Mitchell and Sobczynski both agreed to testify against the couple. Mitchell even claimed that Patty took him on a dry run to the family house one time and ended up having a nasty quarrel with her mother until an aunt showed up unexpectedly.

Both men insisted they had not taken Patty's murderous plans seriously.

A forensic anthropologist concluded that a glove print lifted from the steering wheel of one of the Columbo cars was made by someone with a missing left index finger and the tip of another finger. DeLuca fit that bill perfectly.

However, he continued to insist that neither he nor Patty had anything to do with the slayings. DeLuca agreed to a lie detector test to try and clear his name. The results were inconclusive, but the pharmacist was released from protective custody.

"Hitman" Mitchell also took a polygraph test and passed, but at his own request he was held in protective custody in the witness quarters of Cook County Jail. He was in fear of his life.

Within a few weeks a Cook County grand jury returned criminal indictments against Patty.

She was granted $250,000 bail, but as she had no money she had to remain in custody. DeLuca sat in the spectator section of the court to give his teenage lover moral support and even brought her cigarettes.

In the middle of July, DeLuca was arrested and also indicted on three charges of murder and one count of conspiracy. He was immediately taken into custody.

Like his girlfriends, bail was set at $250,000. He was also unable to raise the necessary funds and remained behind bars.

A series of joint hearings followed during which DeLuca and Patty held hands like lovelorn teenagers. When Columbo complained of feeling cold during one hearing, DeLuca helped her put on a coat.

On September 1, DeLuca wrote a letter to Chief Criminal Court judge Richard J. Fitzgerald seeking the judge's permission for him to marry Patty. They were eventually given permission but the marriage plans then fizzled out.

At the end of March, 1977, just before the trial was due to commence, DeLuca was accused of arranging to have his ex-wife bail out a cellmate so that the man could carry out a twin murder contract on the man and a woman who had worked at DeLuca's pharmacy and intended to testify against their former boss.

That same cellmate claimed DeLuca had confided details of the triple slaying of the Columbo family.

DeLuca's bail was then hurriedly doubled to $500,000 to prevent him getting out to intimidate witnesses. DeLuca was clearly a danger to the community.

A jury of six men and six women were eventually sworn in at Chicago's Criminal Courts Building to preside over the sensational torture murder case.

The judge ruled against allowing 15 homemade pornographic films featuring DeLuca to be used as evidence. But the prosecution was already armed with numerous photos of DeLuca plus a naked Patty and her dog.

Patty continued to claim in her defense that although she had hired the two "hitmen" she had tried to get them to call off the slayings when her father's attitude toward her and DeLuca softened. She insisted she went shopping on the day of the killings, then returned home and was in bed in her apartment by about 11 P.M.—the approximate time that the murders were committed.

So-called hitman Mitchell even gave evidence about how Patty had "wanted it in the ass" when she made her agreement to provide sex and money in exchange for the murders.

He told the court how he'd picked Patty up at a party he had hosted for his friend Sobczynski. She saw his gun in his belt holster. He offered Patty $100 to sleep with his friend. She responded by promising Mitchell she would "fuck his eyes out."

When the so-called hit was agreed upon, Patty asked Mitchell, "What do you want me to do, put my ass on the table?"

"Yes . . . How about tonight?" came the reply.

A few weeks later Patty accompanied Mitchell and his friend to a sex orgy at a hotel and even asked Mitchell where she could get an unmarked gun and some bullets.

Mitchell told the court that Patty had also wanted her brother killed because she feared that when he grew up he would work out that it was her who had killed their parents.

The other hitman, Sobczynski, took the stand and admitted giving Patty a .32 caliber revolver after she claimed she needed protection from her father.

In the dock, DeLuca showed little or no emotion. Occasionally he rubbed his chin and turned to study Patty who was seated a few feet away.

One of DeLuca's own former employees at the drugstore told the court how her boss had told her that two hitmen had let him down so he was planning to have Patty's family killed. When that same witness walked into work one day and noticed scratches on DeLuca's hand he told her, "I took them all down last night."

"He said he shot Mr. Columbo in the back of the head. The bullet came out and took his teeth with it," the woman stated.

Two days after the bodies of the Columbos were discovered DeLuca again bragged about it to his employee.

The witness—who admitted having an earlier romance with DeLuca—told the court that he had threatened to kill her and her family if she talked to police about their conversations.

Then DeLuca's cellmate took the stand to explain how DeLuca had offered him $40,000 to wipe out the two ex-employees before they gave evidence.

On Patty Columbo's twenty-first birthday in June, 1977, her lawyers gave her a birthday card, some perfume, and a devil's food cake with white icing which she shared with some of the officers of the court during a break in proceedings.

Part of the defense case was that DeLuca's cellmate made up the story about being recruited by DeLuca as a hitman in order to get a reduced sentence.

And when DeLuca's ex-wife Marilyn took the stand she claimed she had dinner with DeLuca the night after the murder and didn't notice any cuts on his hands.

Patty Columbo's lawyers decided against calling her to give evidence and she tearfully but stubbornly refused to leave the courtroom while DeLuca took his turn in the stand.

DeLuca strongly denied that he murdered the Columbos. He also denied trying to put murder contracts out on his former employees at the drug store.

He admitted that he and Patty had given the so-called "hitmen" the go-ahead to kill Mr. Columbo because he feared that Columbo was about to do the same to him. He also claimed they tried to call off the contract.

The prosecuting attorney in the case summed up Patty and DeLuca thusly: "They used just about everybody. And in the final analysis, they used each other. Don't let them use you and sail out of this courtroom over the charred remains of Frank Peter Columbo."

After listening to more than seven hours of closing arguments, the jury took only two hours to reach a decision. A few minutes before midnight on Friday, July 1, the clerk of the court read out that both defendants had been found guilty on all counts of murder, conspiracy, and solicitation to commit murder.

The two faces of the illicit lovers dropped. They hugged each other and sobbed.

On August 8, the convicted killers appeared for sentencing. Both continued to insist they were innocent. Standing at the defense table Patty declared, "There is one thing the court cannot take away from me—my father and my mother and my baby brother know that wasn't us in the house that night or morning, or whenever it was, and that is all that matters."

DeLuca told the court, "Patricia and I are innocent. I will stand on my testimony on the witness stand because that was the truth.''

The judge sentenced the two lovers to prison terms from 200 to 300 years on first-degree murder convictions. He also ordered a 20-to-50-year term for Patty, and a 10-to-50-year term for DeLuca on convictions for solicitation to commit murder. The sentences were ordered to run concurrently.

Seven weeks later Patty Columbo was transferred to the custody of the Illinois State Correctional authorities to begin serving her life term. At Dwight she soon became embroiled in more controversy.

In 1979—after two years behind bars—some of her fellow inmates accused her of recruiting them for deviate sex orgies performed for high-ranking male prison officials.

The claims were dismissed by prison authorities as a bunch of lurid unsubstantiated allegations. But they later conceded that Patty had enjoyed privileges not usually available to convicted killers. A woman guard even admitted she worked at the prison for a week before she realized the pretty young woman called ''Trish'' by convict pals was an inmate and not a civilian employee of the prison.

State Corrections Department officials launched an immediate investigation. Several inmates who complained about the alleged sex orgies took lie detector tests and passed.

Illinois Corrections Director Douglas Franzen admitted that investigators had been informed that the parties took place in the basement, in offices, and in various other areas of the prison where privacy was available.

On some occasions more than one inmate was present, and at other times only one woman and one male prison employee reputedly partied. But Franzen insisted the women were not given money, drugs, or liquor but may have received better prison jobs in exchange for their participation.

As a result, Patty Columbo lost her job as a secretary and was transferred to 30 days solitary confinement while a further probe was carried out. Eventually the two male officials and one woman member of staff resigned.

The John Howard Association—a prisoner's advocate group—demanded reforms. Meanwhile prison officials at Dwight described Patty as hurt and bewildered by the claims that she was involved in the so-called orgies.

In 1980 Patty was actually cleared of the accusations. The controversy died down and she began earning high grades while working on a two-year associate of arts degree. She still insisted she did not participate in the brutal slaying of her parents.

She was even eventually given a place at The Cottage in Dwight. But the darkness in her eyes would always remain. She insists she is innocent of the murder of her family to this day.

NINE
Paula

SHE SEEMS PALE, NERVOUS, AND EXTREMELY lacking in self-confidence as she plays with her son and exchanges nervous glances with her ex-husband in the prison visiting room at Dwight. She certainly doesn't look like one of the most coldblooded killers in Illinois history.

Perhaps it's her eyes snapping around the room every now and again that give away the only clues to her crimes. She is concerned that people are watching her when in fact they've all got a lot of problems of their own.

But then Paula Sims's crimes were so bizarre that they would place her firmly near the top of the world's most notorious women killers.

Paula Marie Blew was born into what seemed on the surface to be a normal, happy middle-class family in the Midwest. But there was a vein of tragedy omnipresent throughout her childhood.

Shortly after Paula's birth on May 21, 1959,

her brother was struck down by a severe seizure disorder that meant he could never be left unattended.

When Paula was in second grade the family moved to La Plata, in northeastern Missouri. Her father Orville Blew was employed by the Amoco Oil Company.

Paula soon became known among her friends as a tough-nosed tomboy who "took no shit off anyone." She also expressed no interest in children and admitted she preferred mowing people's lawns to babysitting.

Then in 1976 further tragedy struck the Blew family when Paula's beloved older brother Randy was killed in an automobile accident at the age of 19. He had been sitting next to Paula in the car at the time of the crash.

After that Paula withdrew into herself much more, and her friends and family believe she was never again truly happy with her life.

There were even rumors of an incestuous affair between Paula and brother Randy which might have explained her excessive depression following the crash. But these stories were never substantiated.

The grief-stricken Blews moved from La Plata a month after Randy's death when Orville was transferred to a job at Amoco's refinery in Wood River, Illinois.

After leaving school in 1977, Paula worked in a local food store as a cashier. She was not friendly to customers or staff and was even suspected of slashing the tires of another cashier following an argument in the store.

An unsettling portrait of a young woman with a violent streak began to emerge.

Then in 1980 Paula met Robert Sims. It was virtually love at first sight and the couple eventually married on May 2 1981, less than three weeks before Paula's twenty-second birthday and just three weeks after Robert's twenty-ninth.

In January, 1983, they bought a house in Brighton, Illinois. It wasn't long before Paula was telling friends and family that she wanted to start a family. Robert had a relatively secure job as a shift worker, but he did sleep and work odd hours.

That baby finally arrived in the shape of a daughter called Loralei Marie on June 5 1986.

Twelve days later, as the searing nighttime heat shimmered off the farm fields that covered the pastures surrounding the small farming community of Brighton, Paula Sims was frantically knocking at a neighbor's door to say that her beloved baby had been stolen.

"I was watching the news downstairs when a man with a mask and a gun came in and told me to lay on the floor for ten minutes or he would kill me. So I did. When I heard him leave, I started to run after him and saw that he had taken my baby out of her bassinet. She was gone. I ran outside and I saw a shadow running down the driveway and I heard footsteps in the gravel. I chased him out to the road. But I couldn't see him. He was gone."

The neighbor immediately alerted the police.

Paula seemed understandably upset. She was talking very loudly. She kept putting her hands up to her face and saying, "They stole my baby. We have got to get her back." She rambled on about what a good father Rob was and the plans they had made for the daughter they loved so much.

Paula even said, "I've got to warm Loralei's bottle," and then answered herself by saying, "No, that won't do any good."

At his work, 34-year-old Robert—slim and tall—was shattered by the news. He turned to a workmate and said, "Damn. You're not gonna believe this. Someone just took my baby."

Thirty minutes later he was reunited with his distraught wife.

"Somebody stole our baby, Rob. They took Loralei," Paula told her husband when he arrived home.

"What happened, Paula?"

The couple walked over to the porch away from the prying eyes and ears of the police investigators who'd already arrived at the house. Paula sat down on a bench and picnic table. She buried her face in a towel and began to cry.

Someone asked if Robert's father should be notified. In a flash response, Paula snapped out of her tears and spat out the words, "No, definitely not. He wasn't interested in being a grandfather. He didn't even want to come to the hospital. We're not calling him."

A few moments later, Paula looked up and said, "Rob, I'm so sorry I disappointed you."

He answered softly, "You didn't disappoint me."

"Yes I did. You were disappointed when Loralei was a girl, and I disappointed you because I didn't stop the man from taking her.''

Robert noticed that people were listening to them. He leaned down and whispered in her ear, and she didn't say any more after that.

They never did find the perpetrators of that awful crime and for almost three years the case-book remained open and unsolved. They eventually found Loralei's body in the woods near the house. Charges were never brought against Paula or Robert.

On April 29, 1989, Sheriff Frank Yocom—the chief investigator on that original missing baby case—had an urgent call from police in Alton, some 15 miles away in neighboring Madison County. When he heard the message it sent a shudder right through him.

Yocum put down the receiver and gunned his cruiser down the highway, his mind lost in thoughts of what was awaiting him in Alton. The police had called for Yocom's assistance with an investigation into a reported kidnapping. A woman named Paula Sims had told police that a masked gunman had stolen her infant daughter from the family's home.

Sheriff Frank Yocom already had a very clear idea of who was to blame for the "kidnapping."

It was the second time in three years that this had happened. Yocom shook his head. How could all this be happening again? It seemed beyond belief.

That worn file marked "Loralei Sims" always sat on the table by his desk, and he had always clung to the hope that the case would one day be solved. But he never expected it to end this way.

Here he was, being pulled into a new Sims case. The Simses had moved to Alton since the last "kidnapping" and it wasn't even in his county of jurisdiction. But he knew that there was a chance that this new crime might lead to some answers concerning the original incident.

The new Sims baby case was soon the lead story on TV and in the newspapers. The media's skepticism was immediate and very apparent. Similarities between the two cases were played prominently and described by reporters as "chilling, striking, haunting, and amazing." Robert and Paula were recalled as suspects in Loralei's death, and the press reminded readers that the parents had even flunked lie-detector tests then.

Little Heather's body was eventually found in a trash can. Lacerations on the face implied that she had been smothered to death. Cuts were as a result of something being held against the outside of the mouth and pushing the inside of the lip against the bony gums underneath.

Further examination showed that the baby's body had been kept in a freezer. Early signs of decomposition were inconsistent with the exterior of the body.

Both Paula Sims's daughters—Loralei and Heather—were eventually buried side-by-side in the Woodland Hill Cemetery.

The graveside service was brief. Paula wore a dress for the first time any observer could remember, and Robert wore a three-piece suit.

A television reporter later swore that Paula Sims walked over Loralei's unmarked grave without even a glance.

Many weeks later—after a protracted investigation—Paula Sims was arrested and charged with the murder of her baby daughter. The following day she entered pleas of not guilty on all counts.

At her eventual trial Paula Sims insisted that both her babies had been snatched by a mystery man.

"I want to talk to you about the fellow you saw standing on the stairs in 1986, and the fellow you saw in your backyard in 1989. Did you see any similarities in those two people?" she was asked by an attorney.

"Definitely. It was the same guy," she answered with absolute certainty. No one believed her.

District Attorney Don W. Weber later summed up to the court, "When Paula Sims was smothering that baby, its chest was burning and it was flailing its hands and kicking its legs for two minutes before it went unconscious . . . I wondered if Paula Sims counted every precious little finger and every precious little toe when she was doing that to her. She didn't.

"A baby is a precious gift from God, not a piece of garbage. And I weep for that child who never went to school the first day. She never had her first boyfriend. She never had her first date. She never grew up. She never had a birthday, and never saw a Christmas. The people of the state of Illinois cry for this, and Heather cries out right now for justice.

"Now I don't want you to convict Paula Sims on passion or prejudice. That's not right. And I don't want you to convict her because the people in my country are outraged at what she did. I want you to convict her because there is no reasonable doubt about her guilt; because what she did in her murderous, malignant heart is beyond statement."

Just a few days later—with those emotive words still ringing in her ears—Paula Sims was found guilty of the first-degree murder of little Heather.

She shook her head, dropped her eyes toward her lap as a restrained buzz of whispers ran through the courtroom and the reporters glanced sideways at each other as they scribbled.

The following Wednesday Paula—who had obviously been crying—was brought back into court to hear her fate. She appeared stricken with grief each time any of the attorneys spoke.

Even her own lawyer told the court, "The defendant has told me that she wants to be sentenced to death, and, as a result of that, I believe she is unable to assist in her defense. She couldn't care less what the jury does. She is of the opinion that it doesn't make any difference, that it was all decided before she arrived here."

Paula Sims was sentenced to serve in prison for the rest of her natural life.

She had been spared death and sentenced to life, all on the second birthday of her sole surviving child, Randy, named after her beloved brother.

In July 1990, Robert Sims visited Paula at Dwight to break the news that he wanted a divorce. He also demanded that Paula's name be taken off their daughters' headstone, where it had been engraved below a banner that proclaimed, "Together, Eternally in Love, Mom and Dad." Paula was shattered, and cried for hours after Robert departed.

The new woman in Robert's life was also, bizarrely, called Paula. And by an even stranger twist of fate, this other Paula had pleaded guilty to a misdemeanor charge of battering her 10-year-old daughter. The woman was placed under court supervision and ordered to be kept away from Robert Sims.

In January 1991, Paula and Robert met behind closed courtroom doors for a secret hearing, at which Paula asked for visitation rights with Randy, their only surviving child. She also complained that during calls home from prison, her husband wouldn't allow her to tell Randy that she was his mother. Paula cried once again when she left the hearing.

With their marriage in ruins some investigators still expected Paula to turn on Robert and implicate him in the deaths of their two young daughters. But it has not happened.

But several unavoidable conclusions were eventually reached about Paula that offer some kind of insight into why she killed her children.

1. She had been crushed by the tragedy of her brother Randy's death and perhaps they had been too close.

2. She felt immense guilt over his death and felt that she had inflicted such long-term pain and suffering on her grieving parents.

3. Paula probably felt that to have children would be too much of an emotional upheaval, especially little girls. It seemed that their purpose was simply to cause grief.

4. Paula's love and caring toward her daughters turned into violence when she was subjected to extreme and unrelenting pressure by Robert. She may have buckled under the strain.

5. Paula had very low self-esteem and no reservoir of inner strength when Robert pressured her. If she had married someone less dominating then it could all have been a different story.

District Attorney Don W. Weber concluded that Paula did plan the killings carefully and carried them out ruthlessly and mercilessly.

She certainly regretted her actions but not enough to stop her sitting in her house while Loralei's body lay rotting in the woods 100 feet away in a shallow grave invaded by small animals. It was also not enough to keep her from carting Heather's frozen body around town until it was time to stuff it into a trash bag and dump it in a convenient trash barrel.

There was strong evidence that Paula had planned the murder of her newborn daughter from her hospital bed, and had accidentally let her roommate in on that unimaginable secret.

In the Dwight Correctional Center, Paula remains an enigma—an aberration of motherhood, a riddle with no answer. All that is known is that she murdered both of her infant daughters ruthlessly and without mercy.

And that is a crime in a women's prison that brings little sympathy. Paula never got to The Cottage. Her ex-husband Robert continues to visit her because of her visitation rights with regard to son Randy.

As one Dwight inmate says, "Paula is a weird one. We tend to keep our distance from her. But it's not like being a molester in a male prison. We sort of appreciate the pain and anguish of motherhood, and while we don't understand how she could have done it you can see from the way she is today that she'd rather be dead. She really must care."

Paula Sims has never fully confessed to her crimes so her motives remain a mystery. We can only speculate . . .

A strange twist of fate brought Dwight inmates Kathy Gaultney and Paula Sims together before either of the women had been found guilty of their crimes.

District Attorney Don W. Weber handled the Gaultney case and that of child-killer Sims at virtually the same time.

Kathy Gaultney and Paula Sims got to know each other in the county jail. "I felt sorry for her. She's not a happy person. She is certainly punishing herself for what happened and there's no worse way to suffer,'' recalls Kathy.

Just before their respective cases the women parted with the comment: "See you in Dwight." It was an assumption that they would soon be moving to the women's prison in northern Illinois.

And it came true.

POSTSCRIPT

The Cottage was recently closed down by Dwight officials after a series of incidents involving staff and inmates. This included what officials described as "a serious breach of security." There are currently no plans to reopen The Cottage.

PART THREE

The Central California Women's Facility, Chowchilla, California

LOCATED ON THE FLATLANDS AMONG THE ORange groves and cotton fields of the San Joaquin Valley halfway between Los Angeles and San Francisco, the Central California Women's Facility at Chowchilla seems light-years away from the old rundown penitentiaries that so many male prisoners end up in throughout California. It is also the largest women's prison in the nation.

The compound is nestled on the edge of Chowchilla, among countless almond and alfafa groves growing on dry, arid fields. To the numerous crop dusters that skim through the skies above, the flat gray-and-peach building looks like a giant butterfly.

The prison's cellblocks with their turquoise doors shimmer in the heat haze as visitors drive along the approach road from the main Route 99.

The entrance itself is deceptively pleasant with

a lawn flanked by yellow and purple pansies and red roses. The outbuildings are trimmed with cheerful magenta awnings. But beyond the grass and flowers is a double fence electrified with 50,000 volts, topped by coiled razor wire, and studded with gun towers.

Chowchilla's high-tech exterior—it was built in 1990—has not always operated smoothly despite its electronically controlled cell doors, glassed-in control booths, and modular, semicircular cellblocks.

For this is a place where temperatures often hit an unbearably humid 110 and there are swarms of insects. Tempers are frayed.

"When it's hot, you run out of patience real quick," says one Chowchilla staff member. "Your mood snaps. You get angry. You get fatigued. You get miserable. And you sometimes get violent. Then there's the whiteflies. They drive you fucking crazy."

Beneath the pastel shades Chowchilla is plagued by severe overcrowding, isolation from inmates' families, and allegedly substandard medical care.

And, as in so many other parts of the country, it is predicted that the population of women inmates will grow by more than a third by the year 2000.

The "three strikes" sentencing legislation that exists in California has had as big an impact on women as it has on the male inmates because women have become almost as likely to repeat the most serious felonies. Women *are* carrying out more serious crimes.

"There's women in here who are real evil. I mean they're worse than most guys. They ain't got no future outside and even if they do get out they'll be back here real quick," says one member of staff.

At the softer end of the scale there are also some relatively smalltime offenders, many of whom swear they'll never come back.

One 30-year-old at the end of her second prison term for robbery said that the "three strikes" rule would not bring her back to face a possible life sentence.

"The next time, if I ever do it," she said, "I know I'll never be able to set foot in society again. No way."

Another inmate in for murder but coming close to the end of her 25-year sentence has completely missed her kids' childhood. They only visited her once a year because of the 500-mile round trip from her home in Los Angeles to Chowchilla.

Corrections officials recognize the value of visitation in maintaining family and community ties for inmates but point out that prisons are seldom welcome in the metropolitan areas where most convicts come from.

"We tried diligently to place a prison in Los Angeles," explained one corrections spokeswoman, "and the community fought us in the court system. We would love to have more prisons in metropolitan areas."

But none of that means much to prisoners who've been incarcerated for upwards of 25 years.

"I'm scared about what it's like on the outside," says one long-term inmate, a tough-looking character with a woman's name tattooed on her ankle. "There's AIDS and mobile phones. That's all folk in here seem to talk 'bout. But how am I goin' to survive? I'm just so scared. Those streets have changed, man. The drugs are different. The people are different. Maybe I'm better off inside here."

The prison at Chowchilla is already operating at twice its design capacity of 2,000 inmates. Each room, supposed to hold four women, is jammed with eight inmates who share one toilet, one shower and two sinks. The prison gymnasium has been converted into a dormitory for 112 inmates.

But the inmates' biggest complaint centers around health care. Even prison staff admit that inmates often have to wait three months to see one of the five doctors who serve the 4,000 inmates.

Recently, a coalition of inmates' rights attorneys alleged that medical care was so substandard at Chowchilla that it represented a serious threat to health within the facility. In 1993, the Department of Corrections paid $360,000 to settle a suit over the death of inmate Diana Reyes, 42, who died of acute pancreatitis in 1991, four hours after medical staff found her lying on a mattress on the floor of her isolation cell, caked with feces.

Across California inmate-on-inmate violence is dropping compared with the previous decade but it still remains the most dangerous state in the nation to serve a prison sentence. Officers have shot 36 inmates to death while breaking up fights, more than three times the number killed in all the other major U.S. prison systems combined.

Inside Chowchilla knifings are common and at least one inmate a year is murdered. Guards have been known to kill as well.

Despite construction programs to create additional buildings at Chowchilla the fact remains that the prison is grossly overcrowded. And as the population continues to grow so the already strained system is put under even more severe pressure.

Prisoners' time outside their cells is cut, creating more tension because inmates are being locked up in a small area among sometimes hostile strangers.

Officials inside Chowchilla also have to cope with numerous physically and mentally ill inmates, contentious labor-management relations, and felons who are inevitably going to become more rebellious as their sentences grow longer and privileges are revoked.

"At the point where any individual has nothing to lose, they act out," explains one senior California Department of Corrections official. "That's human nature, but it's creating a tinder-box atmosphere where anything can happen."

At Chowchilla newly imprisoned women, in street clothes or prison-issue blue, stand in sullen line before an intake officer who recognizes many of these inmates from previous visits.

The women, just showered, stand in silence. Their heads bowed. Some of them close to tears while a few of them look ahead defiantly. Nearby, a yellow plastic bin is piled high with clothing that the women have discarded.

Prison officials then assign them a place to sleep even though virtually every place is already filled; cells, day rooms, gyms. In the cells, inmates sleep on bunk beds and mattresses on the floor. In the summer conditions are even worse.

In the gym where so many inmates have makeshift beds, they sleep head-to-head. The women spend their days watching TV, talking, working, and eating. The lucky ones with sufficient education read.

Officials assign jobs depending on what type of crime the inmate has committed, the length of the sentence, and family ties.

But even within a women's facility like Chowchilla there are familiar problems. Among the 4,000 inmates there are unruly groups. Female gangs up from LA stick together and intimidate others. Fights are vicious.

In one recent incident, a 200-pound inmate kicked another woman in the head so hard that the victim went into convulsions. When an overworked officer tried to break it up, his gun misfired, almost killing one inmate.

And these sorts of incidents feed discontent among staff inside Chowchilla as well.

Officers are on constant alert. In one recent six-month period more than a dozen weapons including darts made from sewing needles, toothbrushes welded with razor blades, and sharpened pieces of Plexiglas were discovered.

Staff also uncovered numerous stashes of drugs including balloons of heroin concealed in a bar of soap plus an assortment of home-made hypodermic needles. Ironically heroin is a popular drug inside Chowchilla because it's more difficult to trace in an inmate's bloodstream during random drug testing.

Only 29% of the guards at Chowchilla are women. According to many this fuels the problems of many troubled inmates, some of whom find it difficult to deal with men in anything other than a sexual relationship.

In male prisons inmates rarely become intimate with their keepers. But many women prisoners share their lives with male and female officers shift after shift and friendships are bonded.

In a recent ongoing investigation of state prisons by the Human Rights Watch Women's Rights Project it was discovered that many female inmates experienced some form of custodial sexual misconduct, verbal degradation, rape, sexual assault, and unwarranted visual supervision at prisons such as Chowchilla.

The most difficult inmates are locked up in a secure housing unit away from the main prison buildings. Among those convicts are the members/girlfriends/wives of Mexican Mafia, the Aryan Brotherhood, and lesser known gangs, plus a smattering of others who tend to be serving life for murder.

In Chowchilla, as in every prison throughout the state of California, there are strict rules:

CLOTHING: Denim jeans, blue work shirts, leather shoes. Authorities only recently allowed sneakers.

CANTEEN ITEMS: Cigarettes, soda, vitamins, candy, ice cream, canned food, personal care products, stationery, pens.

CATALOGUE ITEMS: Two mail-order firms specialize in sales to inmates of Corrections-approved clocks, small televisions, radios, tape players, earphones, approved clothing, and personal care items.

EQUIPMENT: Guitar, typewriter, no more than two plug-in appliances, including television, radio, fan, a heating element for warming food and drink.

READING MATERIAL: Law books, most general interest books, magazines.

CABLE TELEVISION: Reception is poor at Chowchilla, so the state provides cable. Prisoners rent and broadcast movies via cable to inmates' sets.

EXERCISE YARDS: Weight piles, softballs, handball and basketball courts, a running track, body bags.

Each Chowchilla inmate's daily diet calls for 3,700 calories: 15% protein, 55% carbohydrates, 30% fat. Here is how much food each inmate is provided annually:

FOOD	ANNUAL POUNDS
Fruits, vegetables	800
Milk	445

Meat, poultry	252
Cereal	200
Fats, oils, sugar	125
Beverages	25

Then there is the typical menu for Chowchilla prisoners:

BREAKFAST: Stewed fruit, hot cereal, scrambled eggs, turkey-ham, muffin with butter, milk, coffee.

LUNCH: Turkey baloney and cheese sandwich, apple, chips, cookies, beverage pack (which when mixed with water makes punch).

DINNER: Salad, beef stew with noodles, canned peas, roll, butter, cake, beverage pack.

At Chowchilla there is a set daily pattern that never alters:

5:00 A.M.: Inmates counted.

6:00: General population wakes up. Inmates with jobs in the kitchen have been up since 4 AM.

6:15: Breakfast.

6:45: Prisoners on medication line up for pills.

7–7:30: Inmate maintenance workers, students report to work classes.

8:00: Medical call.

9:15: Cells unlocked, prisoners with no program go to exercise yard, day rooms or counselling.

11:00: Yard ends. Inmates return to cells.

11:30: Lunch (sack lunch).

Noon: High-security inmates counted.

2:00: Work day ends for inmates with jobs in Prison Industry Authority.

2:30: Cells unlocked, prisoners return to the yard, day rooms.

3:30: Classes end for inmates in education or job training.

3:45: Inmates return from yard, cells locked.

4:30: Mail is distributed, inmates counted.

5:00: Dinner.

6:30: Cells unlocked, inmates return to yard or day rooms.

9:30: Inmates return to cells.

Midnight: Inmates counted.

Welcome to Chowchilla.

TEN
Michelle

MICHELLE CHAPMAN BENDS DOWN AWKWARDLY as she arrives at my table in the visiting hall. We shake hands before I have a chance to get up.

Her weariness is all too apparent although she seems to be putting on a show for a new visitor. In her eyes it is easy to see a never-ending edge of disappointment, yet behind the blur it is clear that a titanic rage still exists.

"So?" she says as she slowly sits down. "I don't know why you'd be interested in anything about me. I'm just another spousal abuser."

In 1991, when Michelle stepped into the receiving cage at the Central California Women's Facility, her doleful eyes stared emptily at the ground. Michelle Chapman was 47, twice divorced, depressed, drinking heavily, and wondering if her life was worth living.

Michelle is far older than the average age in Chowchilla—31—and her biography reads like one of those familiar stories of a law-abiding woman whose life revolved around abusive men, twisted family values, and addiction to trouble.

These days Michelle doesn't often get angry like many of the other inmates.

"I used to have that anger inside me. Sometimes I couldn't control it but it's died. The spirit has faded," she says. "There are many girls in here who feel the world owes them. I just feel I owe the world for taking someone's life in the way that I did."

Michelle doesn't even have to hold down her anger any more.

Disruptive inmates at Chowchilla are assigned to Administrative Segregation or the Security Housing Unit, known as Ad Seg and SHU. Some of Michelle's friends have been frequent visitors to both.

In these special units, shouting is the most familiar noise. Women screech above the already unbearable decibel level of crackling intercoms, TVs blasting in the day rooms, and the nonstop profanities. During Ad Seg and SHU terms many inmates accumulate write-ups, called 115s. Plenty of them are for yelling.

But Michelle Chapman is as quiet as a mouse compared with many of the inmates. She doesn't yell at anyone and she has even managed to avoid the subject of respect—the most emotive word in any prison.

"Respect means little to me because I'm not part of all this. I feel detached. I hate it."

Many of Michelle's fellow inmates are actually proud of being noisy, which often means being on "dog status"—a term that describes being given continual write-ups—110s.

"They go on about respect in here and how you've gotta have it. Well no one bothers me and I ain't got it," she adds softly.

"I feel broken most of the time in here," says Michelle, whose frail features and high cheekbones add an elegance to her neat, pale face.

"I keep out of trouble because I'm not like most of them. I feel depressed much of the time and I don't have the energy or the will power to do anything."

In Chowchilla, other inmates have tried to intimidate Michelle but her lack of response can prove very frustrating.

"They don't know what I am and that's the way I like to keep it."

If someone tries to cause her trouble, Michelle ignores them and walks away. Sometimes they try to publicly humiliate her but it has little effect on Michelle. In the past she has received a "beat-down" from some other "tough guy" prisoners. But these days they mostly leave her to her own devices.

She is doing what she calls straight cell time now—reading novels, spending a lot more time in her cell.

"I prefer it in here. I shut out all the other inmates and lose myself in dreams and fantasies. It's the only way I'm going to survive this place."

Michelle's favorite visitor is her mother. They hold hands and often cry when recalling how life used to be.

When her mother leaves the prison visiting room Michelle is strip-searched.

To be searched, an inmate steps out of her prison-issue clothes and stuffs them in a hole on the search-cell door where a handle should be. Then she spreads her legs while a female officer slides a mirror on the end of a long stick along the floor.

The inmate is then instructed to squat over the mirror and cough. She is also ordered to open her mouth while the officer runs a finger along her gums and under her breasts and through her pubic hair. She folds back her ears and wiggles her toes. Then she bends over, as if to touch her toes, and spreads her buttocks and coughs again. Michelle appreciates it when an officer doesn't stare but some of them do.

From her cell she often hears the freight trains as they scream along the nearby rail tracks virtually every hour—day and night. Other inmates constantly complain, but to Michelle those noises keep her in touch with reality. As do the sounds of the air cooler rattling and buzzing flies and car doors slamming out in the prison parking lot.

She wishes in some ways that she had more friends inside.

"Many of the women in here are younger than me but have lived a much fuller life. That makes it difficult for us to get on."

To even begin to understand Michelle one has to step back and examine her crime.

"You gotta come. I'm gonna kill him. I swear I'm gonna kill him!"

Michelle Chapman was positive that her husband was going to die if the police did not come around to their quiet suburban home and take her away—immediately.

For while tens of thousands of wife-battering cases across the nation are reported every year, this was a complete reversal of roles. Michelle was doing the beating and her husband was the victim.

When officers arrived at the home in Tujunga, near Los Angeles, they took one look at the slightly built mother of two and then at her six-foot, 210-pound husband and shook their heads in bewilderment.

There was no sign of a struggle, no evidence of firearms, and nothing more than an uneasy tension between the couple. And those two officers could not seriously contemplate that Michelle, 46, would possibly harm her husband Thomas, 52.

"Why don't you spend the night with some friends if you and your husband have got problems," urged one officer.

Michelle nodded her head and closed the door to face her drunken husband once more as the two cops drove off.

It was always the same with Michelle Chapman and her husband; the cops would arrive, take one look at them both and conclude—entirely understandably—that she could not possibly be capable of battering her husband. They could not have been more wrong for Michelle was perceptive enough to know that she was on the edge of really brutal violence.

Minutes after the police departed, Michelle got into yet another argument with her husband—this time he was going to pay for it.

As they started yelling at each other, she pushed her drunken, lazy husband onto the floor and began kicking him. He didn't even bother to fight back.

Less than an hour later, filled with remorse just like the most classic spousal abusers, Michelle Chapman called paramedics and shouted, "I hit him and kicked him and he is dead." The battles with her husband were finally over forever.

When the police turned up once again, Michelle made no attempt to deny the truth. "I kicked the fuck out of him," she muttered.

A police officer who arrived at the scene summed it up. "You just don't expect it from a woman. I guess that's why those officers left the house without doing more to prevent it happening."

Neighbors of the couple later said they frequently overheard Chapman beating and threatening her husband. But, as is so often the case, they did nothing.

But what happened on that last fateful day is only the tip of the iceberg as far as Michelle Chapman is concerned. For her extraordinary crime was the culmination of a life that began when she was born into one of the richest families in Beverly Hills, California.

"I started out life with everything anyone could possibly wish to have," Michelle says.

She was brought up by her multimillionairess grandmother—a member of a famous German brewery family—surrounded by servants and went to the finest private schools in Beverly Hills.

Then in the sixties she fell in with a group of hippies and ended up getting involved in drugs. She even went out for a time with one of the world's most famous rock stars. That was the beginning of the end for Michelle.

She says, "I never needed a job because my grandmother provided a trust fund for me to live off. I just fell in with the wrong crowd."

Heavily pregnant, Michelle married a man she hardly knew to ensure the baby had a father. It was a disastrous marriage and ended within months when she walked in on him in bed with another woman.

"I was devastated. I had no job, no career, no husband. I just did not have any direction in life."

Over the next couple of years she blew every penny of her trust fund fortune.

Then she met Vietnam vet Tom Chapman.

"It was love at first sight. I really thought we were meant to live together for the rest of our lives."

But Chapman soon started bullying Michelle and eventually began beating her. One day she decided to give him a taste of his own medicine.

"I was sick of being treated like a piece of meat by Tom so I struck back and hit him. He was so shocked he didn't know what to do and he was so drunk he could not fight back."

From then on, says Michelle, she got control of her marriage by constantly making threats against her husband to make him behave himself.

"He only ever tried to do bad things to me when he was drunk but I always had the upper hand on him because he was always so smashed."

Michelle is not proud of being a husband-batterer but she feels that her husband got what he deserved.

"I suffered like many women before me, but I decided to turn the tables on my man. He had it coming to him.

"There must be hundreds of thousands of women out there who have taken non-stop abuse at the hands of their husbands. Well, my advice is fight back."

Michelle and her mother, Mrs. Pat King, have spent years trying to get her sentence reduced on the basis that Tom Chapman provoked his wife's murderous attack by trying to abuse her.

At the time of her trial in January, 1992, Deputy District Attorney William Holliman said that Michelle Chapman killed her husband by repeatedly kicking him in the head.

Today Michelle says softy, "I can't turn the clock back now, but I do feel that I have been unjustly treated. I only did what anyone would do in the circumstances."

Michelle was actually sentenced to 11 years in prison for beating her husband to death after she had pleaded no contest to the charges.

San Fernando Superior Court Judge Howard J. Schwab said that prosecutors showed compassion for Michelle by not seeking a second-degree murder charge, which would have carried a maximum term of 15 years to life in prison.

"This was a planned killing. She told police she was going to kill him. But I do believe in the interests of justice and compassion that this is appropriate."

Meanwhile Michelle remains in Chowchilla counting the days until she can start to rebuild her life once more.

ELEVEN

Maureen

IN A DIFFERENT PART OF THE FACILITY AT
Chowchilla is a narrow cement walkway known
as "The Freeway" that runs into the two-story
Building 270. It leads to a steel cage with only
nine cells that measure precisely six feet by 11
feet. This is Death Row for women. It holds a
select group of women whose ranks have slowly
increased during the 1990s.

Only four women have been legally put to
death by the state of California since 1893 while
503 men have been executed, most of them by
hanging.

The first woman to die in California's gas
chamber was Juanita Spinelli in 1941. The most
recent was Elizabth Ann Duncan, a 59-year-old
Ventura County woman convicted of hiring two
men to kill her daughter-in-law. She died in the
gas chamber at San Quentin on August 8, 1962.

Today, Chowchilla's Death Row houses inmates such as Maureen McDermott. She does not

fear death, but the spectacle of her execution is what really concerns her. She feels that being put to death in front of staring witnesses is "barbaric."

Maureen, 48—a former registered nurse at County-USC Medical Center—was convicted in 1990 of hiring a co-worker to murder her roommate to collect on a $100,000 mortgage insurance policy.

Now she lives in a cramped cell with few belongings, awaiting her fate.

"There's a great sadness in your heart knowing you're going to die and going to leave the people you love," she says. "But I'm not afraid to die. If they want to murder me, let them murder me. My life is ruined anyway."

The crime committed by Maureen was, according to prosecutors, "a heinous, calculated coldblooded killing." She recruited a hospital orderly to kill her male roommate. The orderly even testified at McDermott's trial that she had wanted him to deliberately mutilate the man, who was gay, so that police would presume it was some kind of crime of passion.

The roommate had escaped an earlier attack by the hospital orderly but a month later he and another accomplice stabbed the man 44 times and cut off his penis.

McDermott was only brought to justice when the orderly decided to give evidence against her in exchange for having the death sentence on him commuted. He got life imprisonment without possibility of parole. His accomplices were promised immunity in exchange for testifying against Maureen.

Maureen says her conviction was "hypocritical."

She described the death penalty as a "joke." She says, "Two people involved in the murder are walking the streets right now. People talk about the death penalty as being just, but how is this just? Shouldn't everyone pay the same price? People in California want to kill people who murder, yet they set murderers free?"

In her cell, Maureen wears a loose-fitting blue frock and a scapular around her neck with pictures of saints. She had no previous criminal record and was considered a skilled and highly conscientious nurse when she was arrested.

Maureen speaks with ease. She is articulate, outspoken, and has a dry wit that borders on the cynical.

There are worse fates than the gas chamber, says Maureen as she takes a slow drag from her cigarette and surveys the prison visiting room.

"What kind of life is this? Waking up every morning to a cement wall is an unbearable future. I sometimes think the gas chamber is better than staring at these walls for the rest of my life."

Following her conviction in Van Nuys Superior Court, Maureen became the first woman on Death Row in California for 15 years. With that unique status she gained a certain level of notoriety. Some of the other inmates at Chowchilla taunted her while others bowed down to her.

"You're going to fry!" was a popular form of greeting.

Says Maureen, "Some of them confused me with a serial killer or they'd accuse me of killing babies or going 'round with some guy chopping the heads off prostitutes."

Then she lights another cigarette and rolls her eyes before wryly commenting, "It didn't bother me that much because you have to consider the source."

Maureen spends her days wandering The Freeway, using exercise equipment, and organizing a small library for inmates. If and when she is executed she will be transported to San Quentin by bus and placed in a holding cell before her long walk to the gas chamber.

"If the time does come for me," says Maureen. "I just hope I'll be able to hold my head up."

But now there are other women on Chowchilla's Death Row. Probably the most outrageous is Mary Ellen . . .

TWELVE
Mary Ellen

AT HER TRIAL MARY ELLEN SAMUELS WAS POR-
trayed as a cold, calculating, cash-obsessed
widow who didn't hesitate to orchestrate two
murders for her own financial gain.

And Mary Ellen certainly combined the trap-
pings of immense wealth with a sexually charged
personal life. She wrote sexually explicit love letters to her bedmates. She even hired male strip-
pers to cavort with her. And then there were her
regular cocaine-snorting sessions.

As a prosecutor at her trial said, "She was
pretty pampered by her husband. Her child was
in private school. I think she had what the average American would consider the good life.
But half of it wasn't going to be good enough
for her."

And as the fifth woman to be sentenced to
death since California resumed capital punishment in 1977, she is certainly one of the star
inmates at Chowchilla.

The 49-year-old grandmother retained her attractive features even behind the bars of the prison's small, grim nine-cell Death Row unit. She refuses to directly refer to the death sentence imposed on her by a court back in September 1994. Whether this is her own brand of self-denial or an attempt to simply avoid the issues at stake only Mary Ellen knows.

Inside Chowchilla, the word is out that Mary Ellen is a sassy woman prepared to manipulate everyone who comes into close contact with her. On her arrival, male guards were persuaded to give up any contact with her on the basis that female staff would find it easier to deal with her.

But Mary Ellen Samuels's early life certainly didn't hint at the ruthless coldblooded killer she was to become.

She enjoyed a perfectly normal childhood that included regular trips to Disneyland and a dearly loved pet dog called Patches. Later, she even taught her stepdaughter how to bake cookies.

Before arriving in Chowchilla's Death Row, Mary Ellen was even considered a ''den mother'' and Bible class leader at the County Jail for women where she was held for four years before her sentencing.

One of Mary Ellen's closest friends inside jail was inmate Gloria Pina. After her release, Gloria attended Mary Ellen's trial daily. Mary Ellen's daughter Nicole—who defied her own lawyer's advice and testified on her mother's behalf during the trial—is another regular visitor to Chowchilla.

But none of these mitigating facts should

cloud the doubt that Mary Ellen is one of the most outrageous female murderers in California's long and twisted criminal history.

Cancun, Mexico, is one of those beachside paradises most people can only dream about. Miles and miles of pure white sand overlooking the Gulf of Mexico. A picturesque whitewashed town with numerous luxurious hotels for wealthy U.S. tourists, plus a scattering of bars and restaurants attractively designed to guarantee hundreds of thousands of visitors each year.

So it was that attractive California brunette Mary Ellen Samuels found herself on a getaway-from-it-all holiday. The perfect picture was completed by the presence of her young lover, who provided the sex and cocaine that had become the staple diet for Mary Ellen.

For the first time in years she felt completely free to do as she pleased. Her boring husband was dead. She no longer had to hide her secret vices from the world.

That evening she opened up a packet of cocaine and chopped out four fat, two-inch lines of cocaine, then pulled out a handful of twenty-dollar bills before finding the crispest note which she expertly rolled into a makeshift straw before snorting her lines hungrily.

"I got an idea," said her lover as he snorted the second of his lines. "Gimme all the cash you got."

Mary Ellen had worked and schemed very hard for her money. She was even carrying $12,000 in cash. That was typical of Mary Ellen.

Her young boyfriend spread a sea of twenty-dollar bills on top of the bed. Mary Ellen smiled and took a deep, excited breath. This was a fantasy come true.

Mary Ellen stripped off her clothes and lay on top of the first layer of notes, then her boyfriend carefully covered her body with the rest of the crispest of the new twenty-dollar bills; she was swimming in money. It was a pleasant sensation.

The woman dubbed by police as the Green Widow was living up to her name.

For Mary Ellen's bizarre sex romp in a sea of money was just part of her celebration following a half a million dollar insurance payout following the apparently tragic murder of her Hollywood cameraman husband by a coldblooded stranger.

Her marriage had originally broken up in 1987 when she moved out, taking the refrigerator and leaving a five-page "Dear John" letter. She moved to a condominium in nearby Reseda, California. For more than a year, Mr. Samuels hoped they might reconcile. At the time he was earning good money as a cameraman on Hollywood films like *Lethal Weapon* and *Heaven Can Wait*.

But reconciliation was far from Mary Ellen's mind. One old family friend, Heidi Dougall, recalled, "She hated him and she wanted him done."

She even told friends that she had calculated she would only receive $30,000 in a divorce settlement as opposed to the $500,000 she knew her husband was worth dead.

Mary Ellen's biggest bone of contention with her husband was over their shared ownership of a sandwich shop in nearby Sherman Oaks. She was also reluctant to wave goodbye to the $1,600 a month in maintenance she was receiving.

During part of 1988, Mary Ellen once again openly told friends she was considering having her husband ''done away with.'' She even approached her daughter's high school friends. She said she wanted revenge for her husband's attempts to molest her daughter.

In one extraordinary incident, daughter Nicole even turned to a friend for help in the school cafeteria. The stunned classmate later gave evidence against Samuels at her trial.

On December 8, 1988, Samuels' husband, 40-year-old Robert B. Samuels was ambushed inside the house the couple had shared until their separation a year earlier.

The burglar shot Samuels in the head with a 16-gauge shotgun. Mary Ellen and her 18-year-old daughter Nicole arrived at the house to find her husband's bloodied corpse and immediately alerted the police.

Mary Ellen later boasted to friends, ''I should have won an Academy Award for my acting performance. I was the perfect, grieving widow.''

Detectives were immediately suspicious because there was no apparent sign of a struggle. It also soon became clear that Mary Ellen was a very spoiled wife. She speedily collected an insurance bonanza of $500,000 and went on a wild spending spree of parties, pals, and drugs.

She splashed out $60,000 for a Porsche, rented stretch limos most weekends, and even took her toyboy to Mexico on that trip to buy a villa in the sun.

But Robert Samuels's death had actually happened after Mary Ellen's hitman James B. Bernstein—a 27-year-old cocaine dealer—had previously failed three times to rub out the unsuspecting Samuels.

The first time Bernstein plotted with Mary Ellen to push Samuels's car off a cliff and then they planned to shoot him after getting him drunk. But each scheme failed at the final hurdle.

Finally, Bernstein had to hire another man to finish off Bob Samuels. That hitman bizarrely shot himself some time later.

Shortly after Samuels's murder, Mary Ellen's former husband Ronnie Lee Jamison contacted investigators to say she had been a compulsive liar who gambled and used drugs during their marriage.

But many more twists in this extraordinary saga were about to come to the surface.

Six months after Bob Samuels's slaying, a botany professor on a nature hike found the body of failed hitman Bernstein dumped in a remote canyon in nearby Ventura County.

Mary Ellen had actually hired two more hitmen, Paul Edwin Gaul and Darell Ray Edwards, to kill Bernstein because he had demanded more money and threatened to go to the police if she did not pay. Mary Ellen paid her replacement hitmen a paltry $5,000 and a packet of drugs for their troubles.

Stupidly, the merry widow insisted on keeping Bernstein's wallet as a souvenir in the glove compartment of her Porsche. Police later found it and also discovered her diary, which stated, "People are saying I did it. Nailed me for Bob, want me for Jim."

After her eventual arrest, Mary Ellen's defense team claimed that Bernstein—who carried a business card calling himself "James R. Bernstein, specialist"—was in love with Mary Ellen Samuels's daughter, Nicole. They insisted he acted on his own when he killed Robert Samuels after Nicole told him that Samuels had molested her and raped her when she was just 12 years old.

Other friends and relatives of the couple insisted that Mary Ellen had arranged the killing of her husband in revenge for his sex attacks on her daughter. No one was ever able to establish if her claims were true.

Prosecutors dismissed the sexual molestation charges as pure fabrication. And Robert Samuels's sister Susan Conroy, said, "It's the ultimate betrayal. He isn't here to defend himself. Bob was a hard working guy and he loved them very much. He would never have done anything to them."

Gaul and Edwards—the men who admitted killing original hitman Bernstein—testified against Mary Ellen Samuels after striking a deal with prosecutors, who agreed to commute any death sentence against them. They were sentenced before her trial to 15 years to life for the murder of Bernstein.

Even though Mary Ellen protested her innocence, the evidence was overwhelming and she was found guilty of two counts of murder, two counts of conspiracy to murder, and two counts of solicitation for murder.

"I've never asked for the death penalty for a woman before," said the prosecutor, who seriously considered filing charges against Nicole, "but these murders were premeditated, six months apart, and motivated purely through greed. Mary Ellen Samuels was a housewife who went shopping for something other suburban housewives don't need. She went shopping for killers!"

The prosecution also told the jury, "I ask you for a verdict of death for all the selfish and inhumane decisions she made in her life. I ask you, ladies and gentlemen, how many bodies does it take? We're talking about murder for the sake of the almighty dollar."

On September 16, 1994, Mary Ellen Samuels was sentenced to death. She will die in the gas chamber or through a lethal injection.

At Chowchilla she continues to protest her innocence and pledges that one day she will get out of Death Row.

THIRTEEN
Cindy

FOR MANY MONTHS DURING 1992 THERE WAS A bulletin board of color snapshots at the Orange County Public Defender's Office that said a lot about one of Chowchilla's most notorious inmates, Cindy Coffman.

The photos included:

- The Fontana vineyard where her first victim was buried.

- Cindy smiling broadly with her attorneys.

- A close-up of her backside tattooed with *Property of Folsom Wolf*, her co-defendant's prison nickname.

- The beaming face of their last victim who was raped and strangled in the tub of a seaside motel.

During Cindy's two murder trials in 1989 and 1992, she wore the same attire each day to the courtroom—a prim pink sweater and a colorful blue dress. But those bright and breezy colors could not hide the darkness of her crimes.

In Chowchilla, the former factory worker and mother of a fifth grader, spends much of her time pacing the tiny cell on Death Row. She fills her days studying history, reading the novels of Danielle Steel.

"I'm afraid of the death penalty ... but I'd hope to go to a better place than here," says Cindy, 35 years of age. "But I'd still rather have life."

Now slim and pretty with her brown wavy hair flowing down her back, Cindy takes great pride in her appearance. Each morning she spends many minutes applying lipstick and mascara. Some of the staff at Chowchilla are thrown by her often cheerful demeanor. She even laughs with ease when asked to talk about her impending death, her six years in captivity, her son and her feelings about the ex-lover who was her partner-in-crime.

She was born Cynthia Haskins and raised in lower middle-class apartments in St. Louis. Her father had left the family home before she turned six. That left her in need of the attention and approval of the wrong type of male.

By the first grade at school Cindy was in psychotherapy because she felt both her parents had abandoned her.

Then her mother remarried a successful executive called William Maender, who adopted

Cindy and her brother and moved them to an upper middle-class St. Louis suburb where the children went to private Catholic school until high school.

In the spring of her sophomore year Cindy smoked her first joint. She graduated from high school pregnant and was a married mom at 18. That marriage fell apart after just over a year.

Cindy struggled to support her son Josh by working a swing-shift at a local carburetor factory. Then she hatched a plan to ditch the child and seek a new life in Page, Arizona, with just a girlfriend in tow.

Her in-laws eventually won legal guardianship to Josh although she was granted visitation rights. However she only ever saw her son once after that.

As one of her closest friends says, "Cindy has to find a man, any man. The truth is that Cindy always had to have a guy around."

Within a month she had hooked up with a runaway con called Doug Huntley and settled in Barstow, California. Even when he was slung in jail in Barstow on bail violation charges Cindy stood by him.

Some time after his arrest another man showed up at her apartment in Barstow and informed Cindy that her lover had been transferred to a different jail. That man was James Gregory Marlow who had just been released from jail himself. Marlow was a strongly built outlaw from Kentucky with a penchant for amphetamines and graphic tattoos that covered most of his muscle-bound body.

Cindy thought Marlow was "nice looking" and they were immediately attracted. Within days the couple were turning up at various high desert haunts. Then they headed east for Kentucky on what was to become a deadly cross-country rampage.

Marlow called her Cynful. She called him Squeeze.

In Kentucky, Cindy and Marlow carried out the execution-style killing of a local drug dealer. Marlow later told cops that he'd shot the man with Cindy's help and they'd been paid $5,000.

As they headed west across country the couple camped outside, slept in their car, and even took part in a biker wedding on top of a Harley-Davidson.

But then Cindy and Marlow began fighting as much as loving. He beat and bit Cindy on numerous occasions. One time he even hacked off her shoulder-length hair. But afterward he always begged her forgiveness and showered Cindy with affection.

In early November, 1986, the couple drove back into Southern California. On November 7 they approached 22-year-old Corinna Novis at a Redlands shopping mall and asked her for a ride. When she hesitated they pulled a gun and forced her to accompany them to the home of one of Marlow's friends. Novis was handcuffed, gagged, and sexually assaulted.

After that Cindy and Marlow together strangled Novis, whose body was later found buried face-down in a field in Fontana, in the San Bernardino Valley.

Three days later Cindy and her lover set off to Orange County in Novis's Honda where they lived off her bank and credit cards and prowled beach towns looking for their next victim. It didn't take long.

On November 12 they spotted another woman who bore a striking resemblance to their previous victim, Novis.

Lynel Murray, a Golden West College student with pretty brown hair and long red fingernails, was working part-time at a Huntington Beach cleaners. She was about to close up when Cindy approached her alone.

After robbing the store, Cindy forced Murray into the Honda where Marlow was waiting. The couple then drove their victim to the Huntington Beach Inn, where Marlow and Cindy beat their victim and blindfolded her before Marlow brutally raped Murray in the shower. They both then strangled her with a towel twisted around her neck. A maid who later arrived to clean the room found her face-down in a full bathtub.

Two days later the couple wiped the Honda clean of fingerprints and abandoned it in the San Bernardino Mountains community of Running Springs.

Police sealed off the area after the discovery of the victim's car and within hours Cindy and Marlow were captured. Both strung out on amphetamines, Marlow was wearing a dress shirt, combat boots, and swimming trunks. Cindy had on a bikini and a big sweater.

At their motel room, investigators found several of Murray's earrings. The couple had taken them as trophies from their grisly crime.

After their arrest, they exchanged passionate love letters from their cells, using sideways hearts to create the letter B and swastikas to dot the I's.

During her trial for the killing of Corinna Novis, Cindy's defense team claimed that she had been brainwashed, starved and beaten by Marlow in order to force her to take part in his orgy of death and destruction.

But witnesses at the trial soon discounted those claims by recalling how Cindy yelled at Marlow in public on a bus, giggled over a wine-and-steak dinner following the Novis murder, and was seen having sex with Marlow in the minutes before victim Murray was kidnapped.

When they were both eventually sentenced to death, Cindy made a point of telling journalists that she had no wish for her former lover Marlow to die.

"I don't want him to die, no," said Cindy. "I understand he has problems . . . I'm very hurt by what he's done to me—it hurt me because of that, but I still don't wish him to die."

In statements made to police after their arrest, Cindy's lover Marlow claimed that the responsibility for the killings was "50–50" between them, and that he was robbing the victims to bankroll a Missouri trip to win back Cindy's son. Cindy even agreed she helped kidnap the victims and used their credit cards, but insisted that Marlow alone sexually assaulted them.

Prosecutors insisted all along that Cindy was equally responsible. Cindy even admitted that she briefly pulled at the towel used to kill Murray, but said she only did so because Marlow threatened to kill her.

She even claimed that Marlow had once told her, "I am the Devil, and I own you."

And Cindy told the judge, "I know I should have done something to stop it. But all I know is, before, I had never done anything real wrong. I don't think I should have to die for my participation in these crimes."

But prosecutors had no doubt that Cindy wanted Novis murdered and that she was the driving force behind the couple's appalling crime rampage.

"She's a very bright woman," said one attorney. "She is very manipulative and very clever, and she *reeked* of sexuality. Oh, you wouldn't believe! She came off as much smarter than Marlow and no one believed this guy was outsmarting her, out-manipulating her."

Before being sentenced Cindy briefly addressed the judge and thanked the court staff for their kindness and also asked the victim's family for forgiveness.

"I just hope that one day the Murrays forgive me," she said in a soft voice. It was the only real humility she ever showed.

Perhaps surprisingly, the mother of victim Murray said after hearing Cindy's appeal, "It's not in my heart yet, but it doesn't mean it won't be."

After Cindy was sentenced to death for the murder of second victim Lynel Murray, the judge told the court, "I have never tried a case in my courtroom where the killing was so debased, so wanton, so senseless, so brutal, and so avoidable.

"It is my hope that the conviction of the jury in this case withstands any and all appellate challenges because it is my belief . . . that you should never return to society."

Meanwhile Deputy District Attorney Robert Gannon described the murder of Murray as "probably one of the most aggravated, horrendous cases that I've come in contact with, let alone prosecuted. Cynthia Coffman is either going to die in the gas chamber . . . or she is going to die in prison."

Despite her crimes it seems unlikely that Cindy Coffman or any of the other women on Death Row in Chowchilla will ever actually be executed.

According to Cleveland State University law professor Victor L. Streib, who carried out a detailed national study of female capital punishment, executions of women are "quite rare."

Since new death penalty statutes were passed in 1973, more than 100 women have been sentenced to death in the United States. But only a very small number have actually been executed.

And of more than 50 female death sentences finally resolved, 98% were reversed, compared with a reversal rate of 75% for men.

Meanwhile Cindy Coffman continues to pass away her time at Chowchilla by studying college degree courses. Her eventual ambition is to teach fellow inmates.

Other than staff and other inmates she sees

across the corridor she spends her time alone. She has become a voracious reader and checks newspapers daily.

She has followed the execution of men closely, expecially the details about how a prisoner actually dies. "This is where you go, This is what happens, and I thought, Oh, my God!" she told one journalist.

Cindy still speaks to her mother once a week on the telephone and exchanges letters monthly with her long-lost, yet beloved, son Josh. It wasn't until he reached his late teens that she even told him what she was in prison for. He had thought she was in custody on drug charges.

Cindy has even tried to analyze why she committed such horrendous crimes: "I'm trying to understand myself, why I did things but I'm still not all the way yet."

Now that Cindy and her partner in crime sit in separate cells facing the death penalty she says they now despise each other.

As San Bernardino deputy district attorney Raymond Haight pointed out, "They were two flaky sociopaths separately. But put them together and it was like Bonnie and Clyde all the way . . ."

FOURTEEN
Ellie

INMATE ELLIE NESLER OPENLY ADMITTED shooting dead another human being but was never even considered as a Death Row prospect. For Ellie is one of the most unique inmates in Chowchilla—if not the entire nation—and her remarkable story needs to be explained from the beginning.

Homemaker Ellie Nesler's life was turned upside down when her seven-year-old son was sexually assaulted by a male warden at a church camp. Daniel Mark Driver, 35, had lured the little boy in the cruelest possible way, toting a Bible and reciting whole verses word for word. In the eyes of Ellie Nesler and her God-fearing family there could be few worse sins to commit in life.

So when Nesler walked into court to hear the case against Driver on April 2, 1993, she felt nothing but anger and hatred. That undoubtedly drove Ellie to commit the ultimate crime.

That morning Nesler's son had awakened sick

to the stomach in anticipation of facing the man he said had haunted his nights for the previous four years. Driver had been charged with seven counts of child molestation involving the Nesler boy and three other young boys then aged 6 to 8.

The child had already told his mother that Driver had threatened to kill his family if he dared tell authorities about the "nasty things Danny did to me."

As the youngster sat outside the one-room courtroom waiting to testify, he could not stop vomiting. And when Driver was escorted past his victim he gave the youngster a chilling smirk.

"I looked up and he was staring at me with this funny grin on his face," the boy later recalled.

At that moment, Ellie Nesler became enraged by the sight of her son's molester and lunged at Driver and had to be dragged away by other family members.

"Ellie's eyes were cracking and her face was flushed," explained cousin Ardala Inks, who was with Nesler at the time. "Her son was puking his guts out, right down to the bile, and this guy had the gall to walk by with this big smart-ass grin."

Nesler recovered her composure and started pacing the floor outside the courtroom trying to comfort her son. Then a mother of one of Driver's other victims came out of the court and told Nesler, "It's going badly in there. I think Driver is going to get off. He got to the kids again."

The court then adjourned for a brief break and

Nesler was led into the courtroom. Sitting at the near side of the table, his back to Nesler, was Danny Driver. Without a word, Nesler pulled out a semi-automatic, drew a breath and emptied the chamber, missing her target only once. He died instantly.

It was only then the full sickening details of how evil Driver invaded the Neslers' life were disclosed.

Nesler's son had attended a summer religious camp in the mountains near their home. Danny Driver worked at the camp as a dishwasher.

The boy and three friends stayed for three weeks but on the trip home with his aunt, Jan Martinez, Nesler's son "seemed very angry and withdrawn."

A few days later the boy confided in his aunt. "He said: 'Auntie, would you keep it a secret if I tell you something?' " Martinez later recalled. " 'That man, Danny did nasty things to me.' I said: 'Honey, that's not a secret Auntie can keep.' "

The boy begged his aunt not to tell anyone. "Danny said he would kill me and my sister and mom if I told," the boy told Martinez.

Within hours of being told, Ellie Nesler took the allegations to the police but Driver had left the area. Over the next three years she kept a constant lookout for Driver as her son grew increasingly depressed and difficult to control.

As Ardala Inks explained, "One minute he was sunny and open, and the next minute he's angry and closed and in your face. He had a short fuse and he couldn't handle the stress of school."

Nesler then sought specialized counseling for her son after he came home several times from school crying and saying he had seen sick and twisted Driver parked in his yellow Buick Riviera outside the school playground.

In 1989, Driver was arrested in the town of Palo Alto for theft, pleaded guilty, and was returned to Jamestown to face the molestation charges.

It then emerged it was not the first time he had been accused of lewd acts with young boys. Five years earlier, he had pleaded not guilty to multiple counts of sex with boys in the San Jose area of California.

He was given probation after the judge at the time was bombarded with letters from Driver's church insisting he had a fine character.

As Ellie Nesler's mother Marie Starr explained, "The system didn't work. We're not violent people. Ellie is sweet, kind, gentle and brave. But when people hurt us, there's a limit to what we can take. I just wish I was sitting in her place 'cause I'm checking out soon. I just wish."

In the weeks following Nesler's blatant act of revenge, a multitude of journalists, talk show, and TV movie people swooped down on the tiny town of Jamestown, California, where Nesler lived.

Nesler, 40, found herself being hailed a heroine and local banks even set up Ellie Nesler defense funds to help her fight murder charges. Shops in the town's tiny main street produced

T-shirts and bumper stickers proclaiming "Nice Shooting, Ellie."

In the outside world the wave of sympathy is undeniable.

A Sacramento bail bondsman even posted Ellie's $500,000 bail.

In August, 1993, Ellie Nesler was found guilty of voluntary manslaughter by a jury in her home county of Tuolumne County, California. Prosecutors had argued for a first-degree murder conviction although Nesler's defense team had pressed for an acquittal.

Three months later, Nesler faced a second trial to determine if she was temporarily insane when she pumped five bullets into Danny Driver. That decision would determine whether she served up to 11 years in prison or a minimum of six months in a mental hospital.

Eventually, she was found to be entirely sane of the killing and sentenced to 10 years for gunning down her son's molester.

In August, 1996, a California state appeals court upheld her conviction despite a plea for her sentence to be cut.

Lauren Weis—Los Angeles deputy district attorney in charge of sexual crimes and child abuse division—says, "Even when a community can sympathize it doesn't make that action justifiable or appropriate. Justice had to be served."

Since being imprisoned at Chowchilla, Ellie Nesler has continued to live by the rules of life that were taught to her from a very young age.

Long before she gunned down her son's molester in court she learned some harsh lessons from her mother and grandmother.

Rely on yourself, she was told, because a woman in the Mother Lode must often go it alone. Trust in the Lord but pack a pistol just in case. And do not seek trouble—but if trouble finds you, strike first.

As Ellie's 70-year-old mother Marie Starr says, "We're like rattlesnakes. You don't know we're there until someone steps on us."

It seems that Ellie has attached the same set of principles to her stay in Chowchilla. Inmates leave her alone most of the time and they tend to only speak to her when she talks to them.

"There is an underlying respect for Ellie here because of what she did. Most of us don't even think she should be in jail in the first place," says one Chowchilla inmate.

Ellie Nesler is well aware that the crime she committed is seen as a bellwether for people fed up with today's crime and today's punishment. It was frontier justice—and it worked.

But then is Ellie Nesler really the vigilante that so many people claim?

On first impression she certainly seemed to fit the bill although vigilantes are certainly a mixed bunch ranging from the noble to the deranged.

Nesler has been compared to the most recent version—Bernhard Goetz, the so-called New York subway vigilante who in 1984 shot four young hoodlums who threatened him.

Without doubt her instincts about Daniel Driver—the man who molested her son—were entirely correct. He had a previous record of similar offenses and was already on the run from another crime when he was shot dead by Nesler. She was convinced that he might escape with his freedom despite the charges against him in relation to Nesler's son and the two other boys.

Nesler was also very impatient with the long period of time it took for the prosecution of Driver to go ahead.

As Nesler served her sentence inside Chowchilla she even managed to sell her rights for a TV movie based on her infamous case. The $110,000 contract with two well-known Hollywood producers risked violating the California state law which prohibited convicted felons from profiting from their crimes.

But in fact the money immediately went to pay the expert witnesses at her trial and her attorney fees.

However, instead of the campaign for her release gaining ground her lawyers heard from a witness that one female juror at Nesler's original trial said she had some information that shed a bad light on Nesler. She said she overheard Nesler's baby-sitter say Nesler was a bad mother who used drugs. "If you only knew what I knew," the juror was alleged to have said, "you would feel differently."

Ellie Nesler, now 46, is scheduled to be released from prison in January 1999. During her trial Nesler had breast cancer which then went into remission. In 1996 it returned.

"But Ellie is a fighter in the true sense. She's not goin' to let this thing beat her," says one Chowchilla inmate.

FIFTEEN
Diana

A SUN-SOAKED BEACH. A PRETTY SEASIDE COMmunity overlooking the Pacific Ocean. It should have been paradise, but Diana Bogdanoff was determined to shatter the peace and serenity, and it landed her in Chowchilla for a very long stretch.

Santa Barbara, California, a beachside town just a few hours north of the sprawling metropolis of Los Angeles and all its well-publicized problems. Local police are always on the lookout for troublemakers entering their little piece of heaven-by-the-sea. But although Santa Barbara is primarily known as a family resort, beneath that wholesome exterior lies a seedy underbelly.

And, according to many locals, those "distasteful" elements include the notorious El Capitan beach a few miles south of the town. El Capitan was a place that people only referred to in hushed tones. You see, it was a good, old-fashioned nudist beach.

Lots of nature lovers regularly sauntered down to the isolated beauty spot and stripped off in a desperate bid for an all-over tan. The majority of visitors to El Capitan were middle-aged. Younger people tended to avoid the place like the plague and there were rumors that the county's perverts could regularly be found watching the nudes through high-powered binoculars.

Phillip Bogdanoff and his pretty wife Diana were two such avid sun worshippers. They loved making the short trip from their mobile home at the El Capitan Beach Ranch Park right across the street to the beach. Phillip had a healthy—some people would say unhealthy—interest in examining the bodies of all those nude beachgoers. He subtly cast his gaze across the perfectly formed muscles and firm thighs of the beach's regulars.

The handsome, rugged, supposedly fun-loving 49-year-old engineer kept himself in pretty good shape. He was proud of his body and relished the opportunity to strip off on the El Capitan beach. He'd been a regular at the beach for many years before he met fair-haired nursing aide Diana in nearby Colefax, California, in 1984. A four-year courtship followed as both had suffered broken marriages so they were understandably cautious about committing to a relationship. Diana also had children from a previous marriage to consider.

The couple eventually married in February, 1989.

Phillip was delighted that Diana had no objection to stripping off in public. He was convinced she rather enjoyed exhibiting her body to the beach population of mostly males.

During the swelteringly hot summer months of 1989, Diana also had other things on her mind. For she was enjoying a passionate affair with the manager of the trailer park whom she had met when he helped them move into their new home.

Diana Bogdanoff found the relationship very exciting, especially since her sex sessions happened in the middle of the day, often while her new husband was lying naked on the nudist beach just a few hundred yards away.

Philip Bogdanoff got his pleasure watching naked bodies. Diana got her enjoyment from performing the real thing. She soon realized her marriage was a sham—something she should never have gotten herself into. She wondered if there was a way out of it. A strange thought came to her as she lay in bed with her lover one day.

"If you wanted to kill someone how would you do it?"

Her secret boyfriend was taken aback. What did she mean?

Diana persisted.

"Come on. A guy like you must know how it can be done."

He didn't respond and tried to change the subject.

But Diana Bogdanoff was deadly serious. As

the weeks passed so her determination to do
something about Phillip grew.

On another occasion as she lay in bed with her
lover she came up with a suggestion.

"I thought about lacing his food with cocaine.
D'you think that'd work?"

He decided to play along with her.

"I doubt it. He'll probably just end up gettin'
high and havin' a great time."

"What about poison? What would be the best
brand to use?"

Diana may have been a very attractive 40-
year-old woman but her lover was starting to
wonder why he'd embarked on an affair with
someone who was growing increasingly obsessed
with killing her husband.

She could not really be that serious about murdering him, surely? But she was so good in bed
he decided to play her along.

"You wanna try getting some of that poison
from those pencil trees that grow out near Morro
Bay."

He could not believe he had just said that. But
Diana's response was even more alarming.

"Hey that's a great idea. Will you come with
me and help me find some?"

Her secret mobile home lover shook his head
vehemently.

"No way. You must be crazy. Forget it. Get
a divorce if you're so unhappy."

Diana got out of bed in a sulky silence, put
her clothes on, and headed out of the one and
only door to that trailer. She was furious that he
would not help her. She would have to find

someone else to help her kill her husband.

Eventually Diana turned to her beautiful 18-year-old daughter Stephanie and told her Phillip was abusing her.

"He's beaten me and abused me more than I can handle. I gotta do something."

The teenager sat riveted by her mother's appalling revelations. How could her stepfather be such a beast?

"You gotta help me kill him. It's the only way," pleaded Diana.

"But mom. You can't murder him. Just get away from him. Leave him."

"But I've got nothing. If I leave him I'll be out on the streets. If we kill him at least I'll get to keep the house and all our money and things."

Stephanie was genuinely worried about her mother's safety at the hands of her supposedly brutal husband. But to murder him did not seem the answer. Diana dropped the subject for the moment, but she'd sown the first seeds of her plan.

On at least three more occasions, Diana called up her daughter at her home 50 miles away in Bakersfield and begged her to help kill her husband.

On the first two occasions she got the same reply, a definite "No way." But on the third attempt, Stephanie sensed the panic in her mother's voice and she gave in.

"I know this isn't right, but if it's the only way then I guess we'll have to do it."

Diana Bogdanoff was so happy. The longer she had spent with Phillip the more she realized how much she hated him. She thought he was a creep the way he stared at all those bodies on the beach and their sex life had faded. He had to go.

Having agreed to help her mother, Stephanie took overall charge of their plan and chose her longtime admirer Raymond Stock to carry out the execution of Phillip Bogdanoff. He was so besotted by the shapely, long-legged teenager that he was prepared to do anything for her.

His obsession for Stephanie was also sweetened by the promise of $10,000 and part-ownership of some property.

The scene was set. Now the besotted lover had to go out and prove he really was the man of her dreams.

Stage one of their murderous scheme involved stealing a car. They then switched its license plates and headed out toward Santa Barbara from Bakersfield. During the one-hour drive, Raymond and Stephanie discussed the fine print of the plan to murder Phillip Bogdanoff.

It was pretty simple really: They'd go to the Bogdanoff mobile home, wait for Phillip to open the door and pump him full of bullets. But Stock was nervous. By the time the couple approached the outskirts of Santa Barbara, he'd decided that blasting Phillip Bogdanoff to death was not such a good idea. There was no way he could do it.

The same thought kept going through Stock's mind: "I'll go to hell if I do this."

When he told Stephanie he was pulling out of it, she was surprisingly calm. They turned the car around and headed back to Bakersfield in total silence. When he dropped her off at her home, she had already decided that she would never see Stock again. If he wouldn't help murder her vicious bully of a stepfather then their relationship was a waste of time.

So pretty Stephanie turned to yet a new admirer called Danny Kaplan, another neighbor from Bakersfield. He later recalled there was something incredibly alluring about the teenager. When she nuzzled up to him and said she needed a favor, he couldn't wait to help. Even after she had explained the task at hand, he took a big gulp and decided to carry out the dirty deed, all in the name of love.

"I loved her so much I'd have done anything for her," said Kaplan. It was a familiar story. Stephanie had that kind of effect on men.

He did not even object when Stephanie said her regular boyfriend, 21-year-old Brian Stafford, would be accompanying them on the murder. Kaplan's love for her was so strong he really believed he would become her only true love in the end.

A few days later this unlikely threesome loaded shotguns and rifles into Kaplan's car and headed back toward Santa Barbara. This time the plan was to blast Phillip Bogdanoff to death as he drove alongside them on the freeway on his way back home from work.

By the time they arrived near the office where Phillip worked, all three were pumped up about their deadly mission. They nervously sat across the street from the main entrance to the building and waited for Phillip Bogdanoff to emerge.

Hours passed by and there was no sign of him.

As darkness fell it dawned on the three would-be killers that maybe he was not even there.

"Let's call it a day. We'll have to think up a different way to do this," barked Stephanie, still very much in charge.

As the two men bundled their mini-armory of weapons back into the trunk of the car, she began trying to work out a different way of killing her "evil" stepfather. But all those hours of waiting had a different kind of effect on Kaplan.

"I'm not going through with it. I can't do it," he muttered as they pulled away.

Stephanie and her boyfriend Brian Stafford were appalled by Kaplan's outburst.

"Come on. You promised. We all agreed," replied Stephanie, who made it all sound more like a schoolyard dare than a mission to murder.

"No way. I cannot murder an innocent man."

"But he's not innocent. He's beaten my mom. He deserves to die."

"You don't know that for sure."

Stephanie tried in vain to persuade Kaplan to change his mind, but to no avail.

Just a few weeks later, on September 21, 1989, Stephanie and her boyfriend Stafford recruited his great pal Ricky Rogers to help murder Phillip Bogdanoff.

This time they headed for the Bogdanoffs' favorite beach at El Capitan.

El Capitan Beach was pretty busy that day. Numerous sun-worshippers lay completely naked in the hot September sun.

Diana and Phillip Bogdanoff found their favorite spot just a few yards from the water's edge. It was the perfect location for him to cast his eyes across the tanned and oiled bodies that lay there soaking up the sunshine. Diana found it difficult to lie still. But then, she did have a lot on her mind that day.

Diana sat up with her knees close to her breasts as she watched the crowds from a distance. Watching. Waiting. Watching. Waiting.

It never once crossed Phillip's mind that Diana was actually looking out for two particular bodies.

The more she looked out for them, the more she caught the attention of the naked men stretched out in the immediate vicinity. One sun-worshipper began giving her the come-on as she gazed past his right shoulder at two men hanging around near the beach wall.

Seeing those men provoked a warm smile as she sat there stark naked. It was 11 A.M. and there were only a few minutes left of Phillip Bogdanoff's life.

She watched as the men began walking in her direction.

"Hey, man. You got a joint?"

Two men were standing directly over the naked figures of Diana and Phillip Bogdanoff blocking the sun from carrying out its duty to give them that essential all-over tan.

"What did you say?"

Phillip was not even sure he had heard them right.

"I said, you got some grass, man?"

Phillip was more a bottle-of-beer type.

"Don't smoke."

Phillip felt anxiety facing these two men. There was something about them. His wife Diana did not move or say anything.

Then the two men looked at each other. One pulled a pistol out of his pants and pointed it straight at Bogdanoff and pulled the trigger.

The bullet ripped through his cheek, spinning him off balance. It was neat but ineffective. Brian Stafford moved closer to his victim and fired again. This time Phillip Bogdanoff's head recoiled and he slumped onto the ground. Limp. Naked. Bloody.

"All I wanted to do was stop his pain," said Brian Stafford later when trying to justify why he fired that second shot.

Back on the beach that day, Diana Bogdanoff screamed in horror. The cold reality of the murder was truly horrific especially since his blood had splattered all over her naked breasts and stomach. She looked down at herself and screamed even louder.

Gunman Stafford coolly and calmly put his weapon away and headed off down the beach with his accomplice. They heard Diana's cries for help and looked around for a moment to see her kneeling naked and bloody over the corpse of her husband—the man she had ordered them to kill.

Police, paramedics, coroners' officers, press and onlookers soon ruined every naked sunbather's day on El Capitan.

Just a few yards from her husband's bloodied corpse sat the shaking figure of Diana Bogdanoff. Wearing a sweater covering her blood-spattered skin, the hysterical widow was comforted by a tourist who'd walked by moments after the shooting.

"They shot my husband. They shot my husband."

She kept repeating the words over and over again. It was an impressive performance. But then, she was genuinely shocked at what had happened.

Through tears, Diana told police about the two strangers who came up to her husband and ended his life just because he told them he did not smoke hash.

"Phillip didn't do anything," she wept. "He didn't say anything to make them angry. He was just sitting there."

Detectives were baffled and they all said how sorry they felt for the 40-year-old grieving widow.

"It seemed a senseless, cruel killing," said one cop on the TV news that night. Some Santa Barbara residents feared that the mystery killers might strike again at any time and any place.

But the only place Brian Stafford and his friend Ricky Rogers were heading was back to their homes in Bakersfield with the beautiful Stephanie sitting between them in the front seat of their hotrod barreling down the freeway.

Stephanie was happy. She'd helped her battered mother get out of a nightmare marriage to a monster. And she'd have a home to live in and a good income from his life insurance.

When the threesome arrived back at Stephanie's home she broke open a few beers and toasted their murderous mission.

Then they switched on the TV and watched avidly as a distressed Diana Bogdanoff poured out her heart and soul to the TV news cameras. She shed more tears, wrung her hands, and gave a wonderfully convincing performance.

The three killers looked on and laughed. It had all gone so smoothly they could hardly believe it had really happened.

"We did it. We did it. We blew the sucker away," said Stephanie.

A few minutes after Ricky Rogers left the house, Stephanie climbed into bed with her athletic lover and switched her attention to a pastime her mother would have definitely approved of.

Detectives Russ Birchim and Fred Ray were seasoned homicide cops who'd investigated just about every type of murder over the years. But the slaying in cold blood of Phillip Bogdanoff truly baffled them.

As one of them said: "No one gets killed over a joint. Certainly not on a nudist beach in broad daylight."

There was only one conclusion as far as they were concerned: Bogdanoff's wife must have been involved.

But Diana was not about to confess to a crime she knew they could not pin on her. As cool as a cucumber, she stuck rigidly to her story about the tragic death of her loving husband.

Neighbors at the El Capitan Ranch Park had only good things to say about the Bogdanoffs. "Nice couple." "Kept to themselves." "Very polite."

Detectives Birchim and Ray plugged away with composite sketches of the two killers based on eyewitness reports. Hundreds of likely looking suspects were pulled in, interrogated, and cleared. The investigation got nowhere for the following month.

Birchim and Ray chewed over a few other possible scenarios. Maybe the two gunmen were a couple of screwballs high on dope? Or was it all a case of mistaken identity?

But whatever their suspicions about the case there was no hard and fast evidence to go on. The two cops were swimming around in the dark.

Then an anonymous caller phoned into a police informants' hotline in Bakersfield and said he had information about the nude beach murder in Santa Barbara.

"I thought the guys were kidding when they told me about it," he explained to an investigator. "Then I saw the newspaper reports and realized they had done it."

The tipster also revealed the names of the people he claimed were involved. The first one on his list was Raymond Stock, the man who carried out the earlier bungled attempt on the life of Phillip Bogdanoff.

Within hours detectives were calling at his home in Bakersfield. He was so surprised by their inquiries that he immediately confessed to his role.

The next person named by that anonymous caller was Danny Kaplan. He had a similar story to tell and gave police the names of Stafford and his pal Ricky Rogers as well as ringleader Stephanie.

Kaplan also told officers that Stafford, Rogers, and Stephanie came back to her apartment after the actual killing bragging about what they had just done.

Within days, the gang of assassins was rounded up. When Diana Bogdanoff returned from a trip to visit relatives in Washington State, the police were at the airport to greet her.

For many months more Diana insisted she was innocent of any involvement in her husband's death. Then her first husband came forward and revealed that when the couple had divorced in 1980, she told him, "You're lucky you're still alive. I tried to hire two men to kill you."

For years Diana had an obsession with killing lovers and husbands.

In March, 1991, at the Santa Barbara County Superior Court, Diana's daughter Stephanie pleaded guilty to second-degree murder and received a 15-year-to-life sentence. Boyfriend Brian Stafford pleaded guilty to first-degree murder and got 33 years after agreeing to testify against Diana Bogdanoff.

Diana Bogdanoff went on trial at the same courthouse, but after many hours of deliberation the jury pronounced a mistrial because they could not agree on a verdict. At her second trial in May, 1991, jurors took just two hours to find her guilty of first-degree murder. She was also found guilty of planning the murder for financial gain and lying in wait for the killing to take place. Under those "special circumstances" she was given an automatic life sentence without parole.

In June, 1991, Ricky Rogers entered a plea of no contest to one charge of voluntary manslaughter. He was sentenced to no more than 10 years in jail because he did not pull the trigger.

For Diana Bogdanoff the women's prison at Chowchilla has become her permanent home for the rest of her life.

SIXTEEN
June

SHE LOOKS OLDER THAN HER 36 YEARS BUT then, inmate June Gravlee grew old the day she married a man more than 30 years her senior. It was a marriage she says was made in hell which was ended by the most drastic measures imaginable.

It was so hot in central California in the early hours of July 17, 1987, that the effort of swinging a ball-peen hammer at 71-year-old Andrew Gravlee caused his assailant to perspire. He hit the old man over and over again until his temple exploded in fragments. Then June Gravlee grabbed a knife from her brother's hands and finished off the job with three stab wounds in the back and one in the chest of her dying husband. To say the attack was emotion-charged would be a gross understatement.

Later that same night, June Gravlee—a well-built woman who looked much older than her 30 years—wrapped her husband's body in a blanket and a tarp, then unceremoniously pushed it into a shallow grave dug in the middle of the rolling, desolate, isolated brown hills near the Gravlee home in Tulare.

Over the following few months June insisted to her husband's worried relatives that they had argued and Andrew had packed his bags and left their house in September, never to return.

Andrew's relatives weren't surprised by the stories of fights because the couple had been shouting at each other for years. But they were puzzled why he had not even bothered to write them a letter to say he was safe and well.

As the months passed they became increasingly anxious about the lack of communication from Andrew. Just after Christmas that year his family decided to call in the police.

Investigators Ron Davis and Bob Bagby from the Tulare Police Department quickly established that nothing had been seen of Andrew for the previous six months. June—short, plump with shoulder-length mousy-blond hair framing outsized plastic-rimmed glasses—did not seem worried about her missing husband.

And as detectives Davis and Bagby interviewed her they noticed the unmistakable aroma of marijuana smoke in the living room of the Gravlee house. They said nothing but made a note to check out her background more closely. Later Davis and Bagby discovered she had been convicted on a misdemeanor welfare fraud charge and had served six days in jail. But that hardly made her a murder suspect.

However the investigators did get a warrant to search June's home for drugs. They were also interested in her brother, whom she said regularly stayed at the house.

His name was Gary LeRoy Smith and he was known to the local police because one evening the previous summer he had been stopped driving a car in Tulare. He was dressed in panty hose, high heels, and a strapless dress.

Just hours before the investigators intended to search the Gravlee home, police stumbled upon the decomposed body of an elderly man in a shallow grave just outside the city boundaries.

The next day, detectives Bagby and Davis rushed to the Gravlee house clutching a photo of the corpse.

"Is this your husband?" they asked June. She insisted it was not. They doubted her answer but could do little else in the circumstances. In fact June was absolutely correct—it turned out that it was *not* Gravlee's body. The detectives were back at square one.

On the morning of January 8 both detectives finally went through with their search of the Gravlee property. They looked for a possible gravesite in the backyard after earlier hearing rumors that Mr. Gravlee had been buried there. But they found nothing.

Inside the house June and her brother Gary were both arrested for possession of drugs, but the investigators wanted to know more about the disappearance of Andrew Gravlee.

June once again admitted arguing with her husband on the night of his "disappearance."

She also insisted he left a note before he left and she showed it to the investigators.

The police then took June and her brother to the local police station for further interrogation. It was there that June broke down and told detectives that her brother had killed her husband.

She claimed the argument with her elderly husband had continued until early in the morning of July 17 and then Gary had got involved. She went to bed and returned some hours later to the kitchen where she found Gary on his own. She claimed he then said, "It's over. Andrew is dead. We've got to get rid of him."

June said that Gary then wrapped her husband's corpse with a blanket and tarp and she helped him carry it out to her brother's truck. They then drove west for about an hour before Gary stopped and buried the body near Kettleman City.

Detectives then confronted June's brother Gary Smith who immediately demanded a lawyer. But the investigators needed more than just the word of June to get a conviction.

First of all they had to find the corpse of Andrew Gravlee. June was vague about the probable location. But at least lawmen found traces of blood in the house which seemed to back up her account of what had happened.

As investigators began interviewing family and friends of the couple a fresh picture of June began to emerge. It turned out that June was sexually undernourished by her elderly husband and she had numerous affairs.

She even picked up men in bars and had sex

with them. One night her husband actually caught her having sex with a biker in the parking lot of one sleazy tavern.

Police began to wonder if June had told them the complete truth about what had happened to her husband. Meanwhile the body of Andrew Gravlee continued to be untraceable.

Eventually a plane with infrared cameras was used to crisscross over 12,000 desolate acres of hills and ravines in a desperate effort to find the corpse.

When that failed the police called in the Department of Agriculture to establish whether soil erosion in the hills might pile a deeper layer of earth on the gravesite. Once again, this proved useless.

Then June admitted forging her husband's signature for Social Security payments—three months after his disappearance. She was told she would be additionally charged with fraud and forgery.

Meanwhile police were getting so desperate to find Gravlee's body that they decided to hire a psychic. The woman was taken by police officers to the Kettleman Hills. But despite enormous efforts the body remained missing.

Back in Tulare it was becoming increasingly clear that June had in fact been directly involved in her husband's murder. Her brother Gary insisted she carried out the killing with him.

On May 26, 1988—10 months after the disappearance of Andrew Gravlee—a preliminary hearing determined that June and her brother Gary Smith should stand trial for first-degree murder.

In June, 1989, Smith entered into a plea bargain that would allow him to plead no contest in return for the preclusion of special circumstances in sentencing. He was ordered to serve from 25 years to life. Smith also agreed to lead detectives to the burial site.

More fruitless days followed because Smith could not pinpoint the precise location. Then the body was found by chance when an investigator noticed some disturbed soil. After a forensic expert had completed examination of the corpse it became clear that two people had murdered Andrew Gravlee.

One person, in front of the victim, had hit him in the temple with a ball-peen hammer while another person, behind him, had stabbed him repeatedly with a large knife. That second person was June Gravlee.

In July 1989, two years after Andrew Gravlee's death, June pleaded guilty to second-degree murder.

But at her trial in February, 1990, that plea was thrown out and she was found guilty of first-degree murder with special circumstances. The jury recommended she be given the death penalty.

Superior Court Judge John P. Moran pondered on the sentence. Only six times since 1981 had California judges disagreed with the jury's recommmendations that a death penalty be imposed. But Judge Moran felt it was imperative to change the sentence to life imprisonment with the possibility of parole.

In prison, June Gravlee cuts a pretty dowdy

figure in her elastic-waisted jeans and ever increasing waistline. She keeps pretty much to herself and few of the other inmates even realize
what crime she committed.

Epilogue

THE LAST X HAS BEEN MARKED ON THE CALENDAR. She has served her time inside. Now she must finish the term back in the outside world she has been cut off from for so long.

Many women become so institutionalized that they just cannot handle the reality of the outside world. The halfway house sometimes provides the answer, but with certain inmates it creates more problems than it solves.

Whatever lies ahead, the female inmate on parole will hopefully leave prison behind forever. But they need family and friends for support because the state handout of a few hundred dollars will not go very far.

Sometimes a woman can get a loan from a service organization or church or from the halfway house. But there's no guarantee. Many will return to a welfare environment and all the problems that go with that.

Yet despite all this, the woman released will

have dreamed about this day for many years. She may be looking forward to seeing her children.

The young woman who went in prison full of hatred might now be a changed person. She may have to learn to adapt once again.

As the bus approaches to take her off to her new life, she's given an emergency number by the prison "in case you can't make it. Good luck. Don't you come back here ever again!"

Settling into the bus seat she looks back and watches as the building she's called home for more than half her life gets smaller and smaller. Now she has to face up to reality.

Will people accept her, knowing she's an ex-con? Will they help her or hinder her? Is she walking back into the same domestic chaos she left all those years earlier?

When the bus reaches her parole destination she gets off and knows for certain that now there is no turning back.

She is one of the lucky ones. Or is she?

WENSLEY CLARKSON HAS BEEN A WRITER
and investigative journalist all his working life.
His career has taken him from local newspapers
to many of the world's most prestigious newspapers and magazines. He is also the author of
fourteen true crime books published in fifteen
countries. He divides his time between homes in
London, Dorset, and Los Angeles.